AR 13 1998

101 BASKETBALL OUT-OF-BOUNDS DRILLS

George Karl
Terry Stotts
Price Johnson

COACHES CHOICE

©1997 Coaches Choice Books. All rights reserved. Printed in the United States.

No part of this book may be reproduced, stored in a retrieval system, or transmitted, in any form or by any means, electronic, mechanical, photocopying, recording, or otherwise, without the prior permission of Sagamore Publishing, Inc.

ISBN: 1-57167-099-8

Book Layout: Michelle Summers
Cover Design: Deborah M. Bellaire and Julie L. Denzer
Diagrams: James Hunt
Developmental Editor: Joanna Wright
Cover Photos: Photos courtesy of the NBA
          Front: Noren Trotman
          Back: Andy Hayt

Coaches Choice Books is an imprint of: Sagamore Publishing, Inc.
                                              P.O. Box 647
                                              Champaign, IL 61824-0647
                                              (217) 359-5940
                                              Fax: (217) 359-5975
                                              Web Site: http//www.sagamorepub.com

CONTENTS

ACKNOWLEDGMENTS

The authors would like to thank John Sullivan for his editorial assistance in helping to write up drills presented in this book. The authors are also grateful for the professional assistance in publishing this book provided by the staff of Coaches Choice Books and Videos—particularly Michelle Summers, Joanna Wright, Debbie Bellaire and Julie Denzer.

Finally, special thanks are extended to all of the players and coaches with whom we have had the opportunity to work with over the years. Their efforts and feedback have helped influence the design and ultimately the selection of the drills included in this book.

DEDICATION

This book is dedicated to our families—who motivated us to strive for excellence and reach for new heights. Their love enriches and energizes us.

George Karl
Terry Stotts
Price Johnson

PREFACE

For the more than three decades that I have been playing and coaching basketball, I have observed countless situations on the court and literally thousands of individuals attempting to play the game to the best of their abilities. Collectively, my experiences have given me an opportunity to evaluate many techniques and fundamentals for playing competitive basketball and a variety of methods for teaching those techniques and fundamentals. In the process, I have come to realize that true learning occurs when there is a need to know, a solid understanding of how to learn exists, and coaches and players realize that a particular goal can be reached.

My co-authors and I wrote this book to provide basketball coaches at all competitive levels with a tool that can enable them to maximize the skills and attributes of their players. As a vehicle for teaching and learning, properly designed drills can have extraordinary value. Each of the four volumes of drills in this series features drills that I have collected, court-tested, and applied over the course of my coaching career. If in the process of using the drills presented in this book coaches are better able to develop the skills of their players, then the effort to write these drill books will have been well worthwhile.

George Karl

DIAGRAM KEY

G	— guard
PG	— point guard
SG	—shooting guard
F	— forward
SF	—small forward
PF	— power forward
C	—center

⟶	—movement of a player
∿∿∿∿∿⟶	—movement of a player dribbling the basketball
⊢	—movement of a player executing a screen
⇢	—movement of the basketball via a pass

CHAPTER 1

BOX SETS

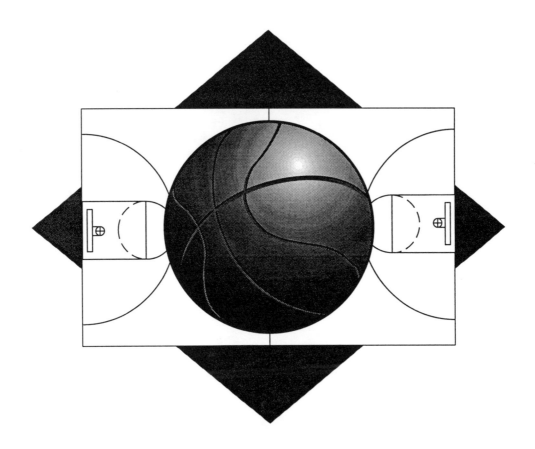

Drill #1: Box to Jumper

Objective: To safely inbound the ball using a box set.

Description: This drill begins with the ball in the small forward's (SF) hands with the rest of the offense positioned as shown in Diagram A. The point guard (PG) moves over to set a screen for the shooting guard (SG). The center (C) sets a secondary screen to pick off SG's defender if he fights through the screen or if there is a switch. SG breaks off the screens looking for the inbound pass and looks for the quick jumper. If it is not open, SG looks to the lane where C has rolled off the screen, or to the power forward (PF) who has cut to the lane from the low post. If this does not produce the desired results, the action continues as illustrated in Diagram B. The C posts up to create a two-player game with SG. After inbounding the ball, SF breaks off a double screen from PG and PF and look for a pass for the quick jump-shot.

Coaching Point:

- The emphasis should be placed on the quality of the screens.

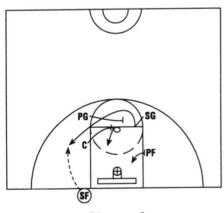

Diagram A

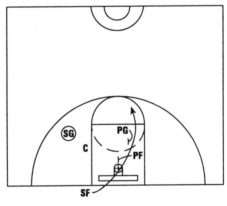

Diagram B

Drill #2: Big Screens Little

Objective: To safely inbound the ball using a box set.

Description: In this drill, the ball is inbounded by the shooting guard (SG). The drill begins with the players positioned as shown in Diagram A. The post players begin the drill by crossing through the lane. As they cross, the power forward (PF) attempts to hinder the movement of the center's (C) defender. As C crosses the lane toward the small forward (SF), SF loops around to the foul line and sets a solid screen for the point guard (PG). PG cuts off the screen to the ballside wing to look for the inbound pass. SF completes the play by rolling off the screen to look for a pass in the lane. Diagrams B and C illustrate options to use after inbounding the ball. In Diagram B, PG receives the ball and passes back to SF. PF then screens for SG, who cuts to the offside wing looking for a pass from SF to take the quick jumper. If the shot is not open, SG tries to feed the PF near the basket. If that is not open, C breaks across the lane to the high post looking for a pass from SG as shown in Diagram C.

Coaching Point:

• The need to be discreet in his attempts to hinder the progress of C's defender should be stressed to PF.

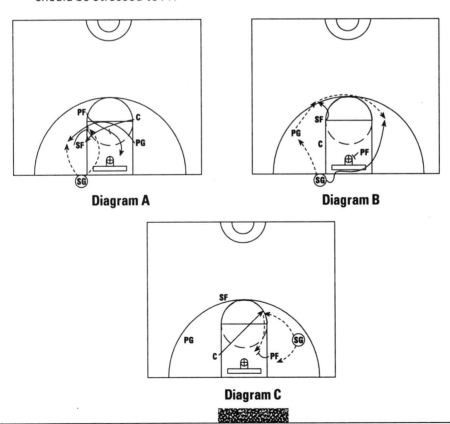

Diagram A   **Diagram B**

Diagram C

Drill #3: Posting Up the Point

Objective: To safely inbound the ball using a box set; to benefit from a height advantage for the point guard.

Description: This drill begins with the ball in the point guard's (PG) hands and the rest of the offense positioned as shown in Diagram A. The power forward (PF) breaks quickly to the corner for the pass from PG. PG then breaks inbounds and establishes good low post position on his opponent. PF immediately looks to get the ball into PG to take advantage of the size discrepancy. If PF is unable to get the ball in, the shooting guard (SG) breaks to the wing to receive a pass from PF. PG then moves out to set a backscreen for PF who cuts off the pick to the lane for a pass from SG. Diagrams B and C illustrate other options. If SG does not get the ball to PF immediately, PF continues through the lane, and breaks off a double screen set on the offside by the small forward (SF) and the center (C). As PF receives the pass, SF rolls off the screen to the lane, and C breaks low to receive a lob pass as shown in Diagram B. In Diagram C, PF downscreens for PG and rolls off the pick into good post position. C breaks from the offside through the lane to the foul line, giving SG three passing options.

Coaching Point:

- Even if a size advantage does not exist, this maneuver is a good play to use if the PG plays well with his back to the basket.

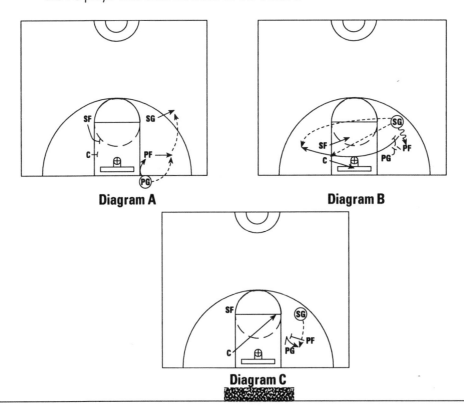

Diagram A   Diagram B

Diagram C

Drill #4: Screen Once, Screen Twice

Objective: To safely inbound the ball using a box set.

Description: This drill begins with the small forward (SF) inbounding the ball and the rest of the offense positioned as shown in Diagram A. Both post players break up the lane and set screens for the point guard (PG) and shooting guard (SG). Both guards cut hard to the baseline looking for the pass from SF, with PG the primary target. The center (C) sets another screen, this time moving across the lane to pick off the power forward's (PF) defender. Both post players work to get open for the pass inside. After receiving the inbound pass, PG can take the quick shot or look to pass inside. If SF cannot get the ball to PG, PF and C become secondary targets as shown in Diagram B. If PG elects not to shoot, or is unable to get a quick pass to the PF or C, action continues as shown in Diagram C. The PF and C set a double screen for SF who curls off the pick looking for a pass from PG.

Coaching Point:

- Emphasize to both guards the importance of decoying their defenders before cutting off the initial screens.

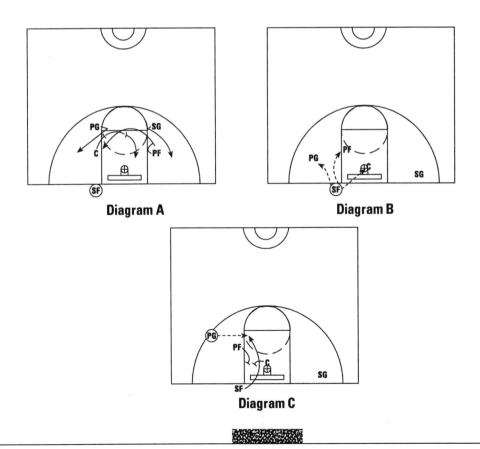

Diagram A   Diagram B

Diagram C

Drill #5: Box Cross

Objective: To safely inbound the ball using a box set.

Description: This drill begins with the small forward (SF) inbounding the ball and the rest of the offense positioned as shown in Diagram A. The point guard (PG) and the center (C) cross through the lane. The C receives the inbound pass from SF, who then moves outside to set up a possible two-player game between C and the shooting guard (SG). If that is not available, the action continues as shown in Diagram B, with the power forward (PF) breaking through the lane to receive a pass from C. As PF receives the pass, SG moves out to set a backscreen for C. C then cuts to the lane looking for a pass from PF. PF has the option of hitting C quickly, or passing cross court to PG, who looks inside to find C continuing across the lane as illustrated in Diagram C. If C cannot get the ball to PF breaking through the lane, he has the option to pass out to SF on the perimeter. Then, as shown in Diagram D, C can set a pick for SG, who pops out looking for the pass and a quick shot. If the shot is not open, a two-player game can take place between C and SG.

Coaching Point:

- The PF should either hit C quickly off the screen or reverse the ball to PG immediately. Quick decision making and rapid ball movement by PF are crucial.

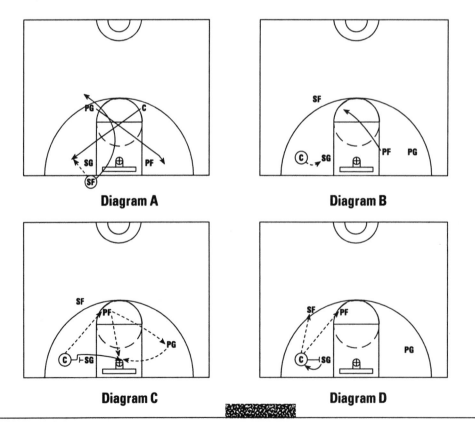

Diagram A	Diagram B
Diagram C	Diagram D

Drill #6: Free the SG

Objective: To safely inbound the ball using a box set; to get the ball into the hands of a team's best shooter for a quick jump-shot.

Description: The drill begins with the ball in the small forward's (SF) hands and the rest of the offense positioned as shown in Diagram A. The center (C) moves up the lane to screen for the point guard (PG), who cuts off the screen to receive the inbound pass. C then moves across the lane to set a double screen with the power forward (PF). The shooting guard (SG) uses the double screen to break up the lane for the pass from PG, and looks for a quick jump-shot from the foul line area. If the shot is not open, play continues as illustrated in Diagram B. SF breaks off a screen set by PF, and C posts up in the lane. SG can find C on the post, PF down low, or SF on the wing.

Coaching Point:

• The coach should emphasize to SG the need to set up his defender before cutting off the double screen.

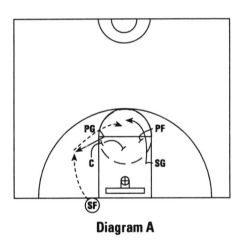

Diagram A

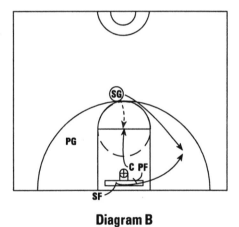

Diagram B

Drill #7: Box to One-on-One

Objective: To safely inbound the ball using a box set; to set up a one-on-one situation for the small forward.

Description: The drill begins with the ball in the small forward's(SF) hands and the rest of the offense positioned as shown in Diagram A. The power forward (PF) moves up to set a screen for the center (C). C cuts off the screen to receive the inbound pass and immediately passes out to the point guard (PG) who has broken cross court. C then moves to the offside wing. After inbounding the ball, SF establishes a solid post-up position on his defender. The ball is moved rapidly around the perimeter with SF sliding through the lane and looking for the pass. C then finds SF in the post (Diagram B), and the one-on-one game between SF and his defender commences.

Coaching Points:

- The coach should emphasize to the perimeter players the need to occupy their defenders to prevent SF's defender from getting too much help. The perimeter players should stay wide.

- This play can be used to set up a one-on-one situation for any player. It is an especially effective maneuver for guards who have a size advantage over their defenders.

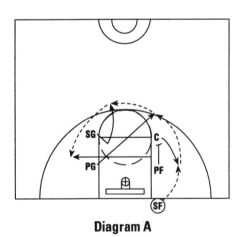

Diagram A

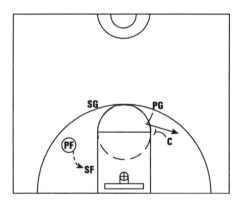

Diagram B

Drill #8: Free the SF

Objective: To safely inbound the ball using a box set.

Description: This drill is designed to free the small forward (SF) after he inbounds the ball. Players should be positioned as shown in Diagram A. The center (C) breaks quickly to the corner to receive the inbound pass. The point guard (PG) crosses over to screen for the shooting guard (SG) and then continues down to team up with the power forward (PF). SG breaks off the screen and receives a pass from C. C immediately sets a screen for SF (Diagram B) who pops out to receive a pass from SG. SF's other option is to fake as if to break off C's screen, then reverse direction across the baseline to work off the double screen set by PG and PF.

Coaching Point:

• This play is most effective when the small forward is a good outside shooter. It clears out the middle and leaves SG free to make a one-on-one drive to the basket.

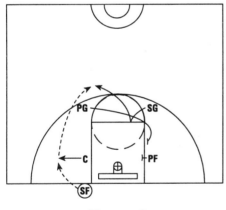

Diagram A

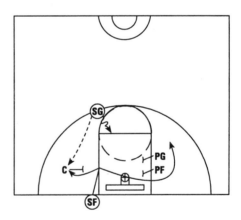

Diagram B

Drill #9: Lob Drill

Objective: To safely inbound the ball using a box set; to practice executing a lob pass.

Description: This drill begins with the small forward (SF) inbounding the ball and the rest of the offense positioned as shown in Diagram A. The center (C) breaks to the corner to take the inbound pass and immediately passes to the point guard (PG) near the top of the key. The shooting guard (SG) moves down to set a screen for the power forward (PF). PF breaks off the screen to the top of the key to receive a pass from PG. After inbounding the ball, SF sets a backscreen for C. C cuts off the screen along the baseline toward the basket and looks to receive a lob pass from PF. If the lob isn't open, PF passes to SG on the wing, and sets a double screen with PG for the SF (Diagram B). SF breaks off the screen to the top of the key for a pass from SG and a jump-shot. Diagram C illustrates the next option if SF can't take the jumper. C moves from the low post to the foul line, clearing the way for SG to try a backdoor move. PF screens down to free PG for a jumper. SF can either find SG going backdoor or pass to PG for the shot. PF rolls to the hoop off the pick, giving PG another option.

Coaching Point:

• Quick movement from one option to the next should be emphasized.

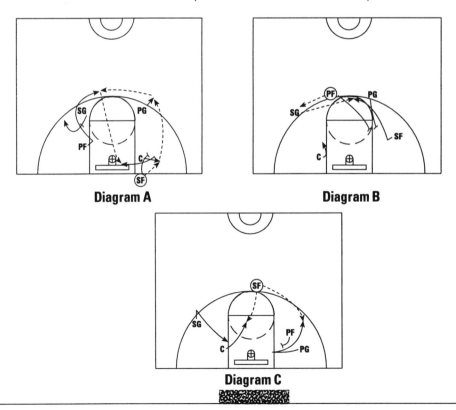

Diagram A   **Diagram B**

Diagram C

Drill #10: Spread the "D"

Objective: To safely inbound the ball using a box set; to spread the defense to facilitate getting the ball in the lane.

Description: The drill begins with the small forward (SF) inbounding the ball and the rest of the offense positioned as shown in Diagram A. The center (C) and power forward (PF) cross up the lane to screen for the shooting guard (SG) and the point guard (PG). After screening for SG, C cuts down to the wing to receive the inbound pass. In Diagram B, both guards move to the offside, and PF is positioned near the top of the key. After inbounding the ball, SF posts up looking for a quick pass from C. The defense is spread, giving SF a good one-on-one opportunity. If C cannot get the ball in to SF, SG comes up to backscreen for PF at the top of the key (Diagram C). PF cuts down the lane off the screen looking for a pass from C.

Coaching Point:

• The coach should emphasize to SG and PG the need to stay wide on the offside to open up the floor.

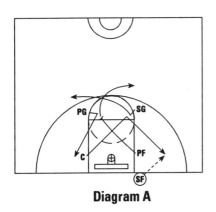

Diagram A

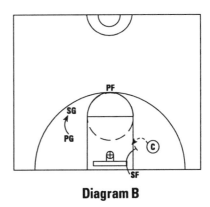

Diagram B

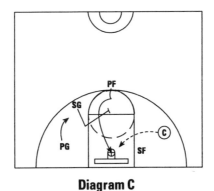

Diagram C

Drill #11: Post Up or Lob Drill

Objective: To safely inbound the ball using a box set.

Description: The drill begins with the ball in the small forward's (SF) hands and the rest of the offense positioned as shown in Diagram A. The center (C) breaks to the corner to receive the inbound pass, and SF immediately establishes a good post- up position on his defender. C attempts to get the ball into the post so SF can work one-on-one. If C can't get the ball into the post, the shooting guard (SG) sets a backscreen for the power forward (PF). PF breaks around the screen and moves down the lane looking for a lob pass from C. If the lob is not open, C passes to SG near the foul line. SG takes the quick jump-shot if it is open. If not, SG attempts to work the ball into PF who has established a post-up position. If all of the above fail, the action continues as illustrated in Diagram B. SF crosses the lane to screen for PF, who moves off the screen to post up on the opposite side of the lane. After screening for PF, SF breaks to the foul line looking for a pass to take the jumper.

Coaching Points:

- The importance of   establishing good post-up position should be emphasized.
- The coach should insist that the lob pass option be practiced during the drill.

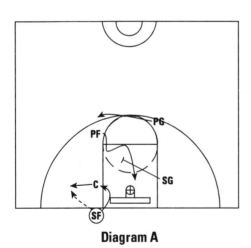

Diagram A

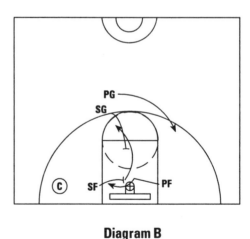

Diagram B

Drill #12: Quick Score Drill

Objective: To safely inbound the ball using a box set; to create an instant scoring opportunity.

Description: This drill begins with the small forward (SF) inbounding the ball and the rest of the offense positioned as shown in the diagram below. The center (C) moves diagonally up the lane to set a screen for the shooting guard (SG). As the point guard (PG) clears to the sideline, SG breaks off the screen to the ballside wing. The power forward (PF) sets a backscreen for C. C cuts outside off the screen to the basket, and PF rolls toward the inbounder. This gives SF three options for a quick score on the inbound pass. If none are available, PG is on the deep sideline as a safe alternative.

Coaching Point:

- It should be emphasized to SG, C, and PF the importance of getting a quick shot if they receive a pass.

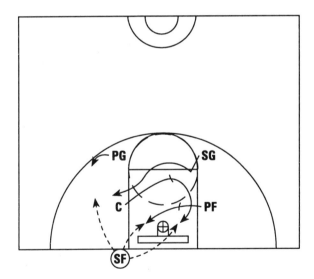

Drill #13: Double Up

Objective: To safely inbound the ball; to create scoring opportunities against a man-to-man defense.

Description: The drill begins with the ball in the small forward's (SF) hands and the offense positioned as shown in Diagram A. Both post players move up the lane to set screens for the shooting guard (SG) and the point guard (PG). SG breaks off the screen by the center (C) and receives the inbound pass. Then, as shown in Diagram B, SF moves up the lane to set a screen for the power forward (PF), who breaks off the screen to the low post. The C then slides across the lane and sets a screen for SF. SF cuts off the screen to the ballside for a pass to take the short jumper. This play is designed to create three options for SG. He may take the quick jumper after receiving the inbound pass, or look either to PF down low or SF outside.

Coaching Point:

- This play is especially effective against teams who like to play close man-to-man defense.

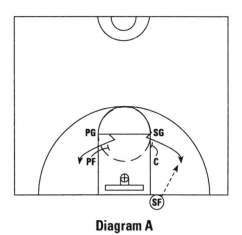

Diagram A

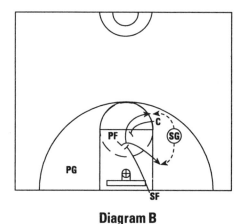

Diagram B

Drill #14: Little Inside, Big Outside

Objective: To safely inbound the ball using a box set.

Description: This drill begins with the ball in the hands of the small forward (SF) and the rest of the offense positioned as shown in Diagram A. The point guard (PG) moves across the lane and takes his place in tandem with the shooting guard (SG) in the low post. The power forward (PF) moves across the top of the lane to screen for the center (C). C breaks off the screen to the ballside wing to take the inbound pass, and PF rolls off the pick to the top of the key. On receiving the pass, C immediately reverses the ball to PF. The players should now be positioned as shown in Diagram B. With the entire weakside of the court open, the inbounder sprints to the wing in an effort to get his defender chasing out of control. If successful, SF attempts a backdoor move to the lane. At the same time, C and PG set a double screen for SG. SG loops around the screen to the lane, giving PF a second passing option.

Coaching Point:

- This play is especially effective against tight man-to-man defenses.

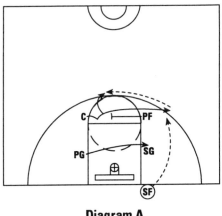

Diagram A

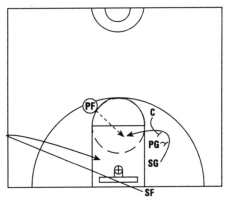

Diagram B

Drill #15: Free the C

Objective: To safely inbound the ball using a box set.

Description: This drill begins with the point guard (PG) inbounding the ball and the rest of the offense positioned as shown in Diagram A. The power forward (PF) crosses the key toward the ball, then cuts up the lane to the high ballside wing. As PF crosses the key, the small forward (SF) and the center (C) move in the opposite direction and set a double screen for the shooting guard (SG). SG breaks off the double screen to the ballside low wing to receive the inbound pass. After screening for SG, SF moves back toward the ball as a safety, and C takes a position opposite PF on the high wing. After inbounding the ball, PG breaks up the lane and sets a backscreen for C. C v-cuts down the lane off the pick to receive a pass from PF. SG and SF keep their defenders busy on the perimeter to avoid defensive sagging to the middle (Diagram B). If PG sets a solid screen, C should be wide open in the lane. If the defense switches, a size advantage is created, allowing a lob pass. Diagram C illustrates another option if C does not get free off the pick. PF dribbles toward PG, who breaks off the screen to receive a pass. C continues down the lane and loops back to establish a good low post position on his defender. PG attempts to get the ball into C on the low post.

Coaching Point:

- The emphasis should be on PG setting a good screen and on C decoying his defender before cutting off the pick.

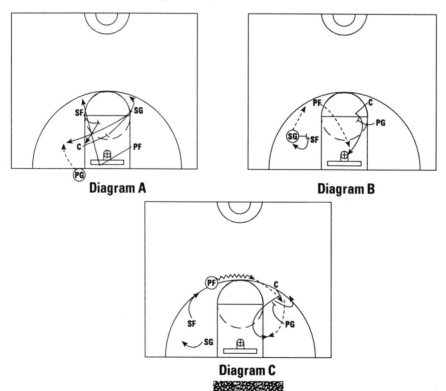

Diagram A

Diagram B

Diagram C

Drill #16: Perimeter Triple Threat

Objective: To safely inbound the ball using a box set; to create a scoring opportunity for any of three perimeter players.

Description: The drill begins with the players positioned as shown in Diagram A. The power forward (PF) breaks across the lane, driving his defender into a double screen set by the center (C) and shooting guard (SG). PF catches the inbound pass and immediately passes to SG, who has rolled to the perimeter. After inbounding the ball, the small forward (SF) breaks to the opposite wing. The point guard (PG) sets a pick in the lane to free SF for a pass from SG and the quick jump-shot. If the shot is not open, C moves up the lane to set a screen for SG. SG cuts off the pick across the lane with help from a second screen set by PG (Diagram B). If SG has a size advantage over the defender, he may stop and post up, or continue to the wing, looking for the pass from SF and the shot. If SG does not get open for the pass, C and PF set a barricade screen in the lane for PG. PG cuts off the screen to the perimeter to receive the pass and take the jumper (Diagram C).

Coaching Point:

- The coach should emphasize moving from one option to the next as quickly as possible.

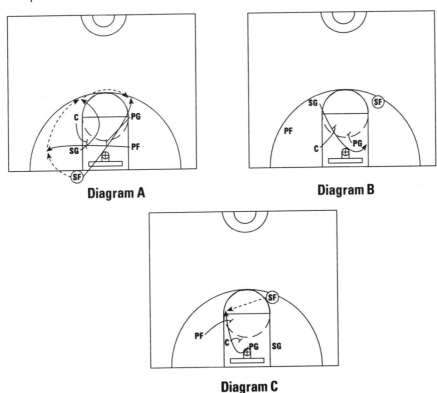

Diagram A

Diagram B

Diagram C

Drill #17: Power Box

Objective: To safely inbound the ball using a box set; to provide an opportunity for dominant inside players to overpower their defenders.

Description: This drill begins with the players positioned as shown in Diagram A. The power forward (PF) breaks to the sideline to take the inbound pass, and the small forward (SF) clears to the top of the key. The point guard (PG) v-cuts to get open on the wing to receive a pass from PF. The center (C) breaks across the lane and establishes a good post up position on his defender. All three perimeter players are out high, leaving PF and C alone on the baseline. PF can feed the ball into C, or begin a two-on-two game with C. If neither option is open, PF passes out to PG who moves the ball to SF at the tops of the key (Diagram B). C then sets a pick for PF and rolls to the basket after screening. PF sets up his defender with a v-cut and breaks off the screen across the lane. If the defense switches, SF can find C sealing off the lane. If the defense remains in a man-to-man, PF should be ahead of the defender breaking across the lane.

Coaching Point:

- It should be emphasized to the post players that this play is designed to let them use their best power moves.

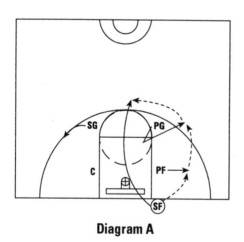

Diagram A

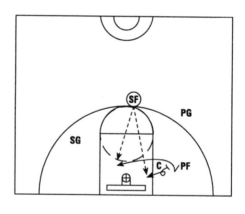

Diagram B

Drill #18: Big Picks Little, Big Picks Big

Objective: To safely inbound the ball using a box set.

Description: The drill begins with the ball in the small forward's (SF) hands and the players positioned as shown in the diagram below. It is designed to use two big strong bodies to set two screens and free teammates for the inbound pass. The power forward (PF) moves up the lane to set a pick for the shooting guard (SG). SG cuts off the screen to the open wing looking for the pass. The center (C) crosses the lane to set a screen for PF, who breaks off the pick toward the basket to give SF a second option for the inbound pass. After screening, C rolls back toward SF, creating a third inbound option. The point guard (PG) remains high to act as a safety if none of the first three options are available.

Coaching Point:

- This play is designed to force defenders to decide whether to stay with their man or switch. Any miscommunication should result in an offensive advantage.

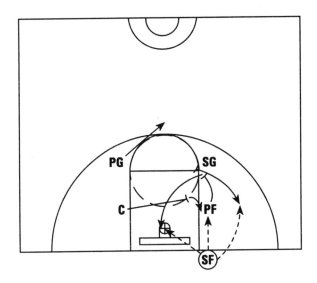

Drill #19: Double Reverse Drill

Objective: To safely inbound the ball using a box set.

Description: The drill begins with the point guard (PG) inbounding the ball and the rest of the offense positioned as shown in Diagram A. The small forward (SF) screens for the shooting guard (SG), who cuts off the pick to the ballside wing for the inbound pass. SF then moves down the lane to set a double screen with the center (C) for the power forward (PF). The PF cuts off the screen to the high ballside wing. After screening, SF moves back to the high post, and C rolls out to the offside high wing. PG moves to the offside wing after inbounding the ball. As the ball is reversed around the perimeter, SF moves up to set a backscreen for PF. When the ball is reversed to C, he dribbles slowly toward PG. As PF cuts through the lane off the screen, C looks to see if PF is open for a pass (Diagram B). If not, PG also screens for PF. SF follows the action down the lane and sets a second screen for PG, who curls around the pick for a pass from C and the short jumper. If no shot is available, C passes to PF, who moves to the corner, and a two-person game with the post players commences (Diagram C). C posts up low, and PF attempts to get the ball inside. If unable to feed the ball into C, PF reverses the ball around the perimeter for the second time (Diagram D). C then moves out to set a backscreen for PF, who cuts off the pick to the basket looking for a pass from SG.

Coaching Point:

- Rapid ball movement around the perimeter and quickly flowing from one option to the next should be emphasized.

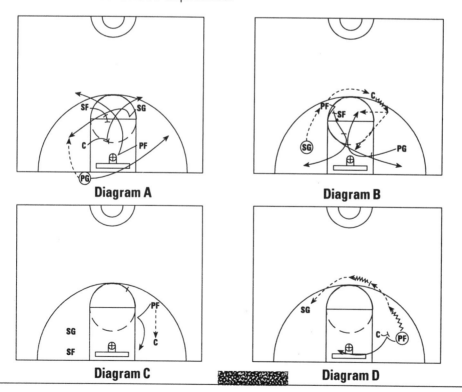

Diagram A

Diagram B

Diagram C

Diagram D

Drill #20: Read PG's Defender

Objective: To safely inbound the ball using a box set.

Description: The drill begins with the players positioned as shown in Diagram A. The small forward (SF) and shooting guard (SG) move down the lane to set a screen for the center (C). C breaks off the screen to the ballside top of the key, and the power forward (PF) crosses the lane looking for the inbound pass under the basket. If PF does not get the pass, he breaks up the lane to the offside top of the key. SG breaks to the wing to receive the inbound pass (Diagram B), then reverses the ball through C to PF. After inbounding, the point guard (PG) breaks hard to the offside wing. If PG's opponent is playing tight man-to-man defense, PG goes backdoor looking for the pass from PF. If the backdoor is not available, PF passes to PG on the wing. SF and C have been reading PG's defender, and when the ball moves to PG on the wing, SF sets a backscreen for C, who cuts across the lane for a pass from PG (Diagram C).

Coaching Point:

- It should be emphasized to SF and C the importance of delaying the backscreen and cut down the lane until they are sure PG does not have the backdoor move open.

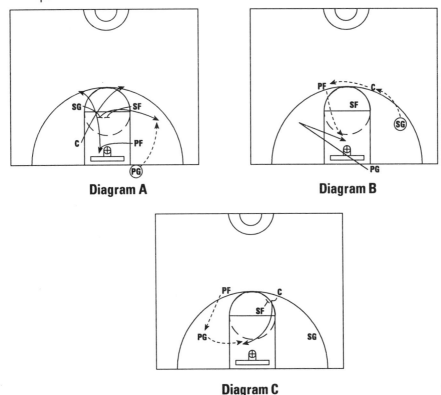

Diagram A   **Diagram B**

Diagram C

Drill #21: Clear It Out and Lob

Objective: To safely inbound the ball using a box set.

Description: The drill begins with the players positioned as shown in Diagram A. The power forward (PF) breaks toward the sideline to take the inbound pass, then quickly passes to the point guard (PG), who passes to the shooting guard (SG). The center (C) clears out the offside defense by breaking up the lane looking for a pass from SG. After inbounding the ball, the small forward (SF) sets a solid backscreen for PF. PF sets up his defender with a v-cut, and breaks off the pick along the baseline looking for the lob pass from SG (Diagram B).

Coaching Point:

• The SG should be instructed to dribble in position to get a better angle for the lob pass and to improve the timing of the pass.

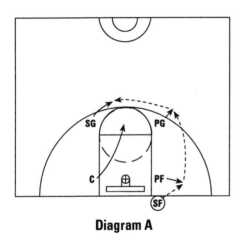

Diagram A

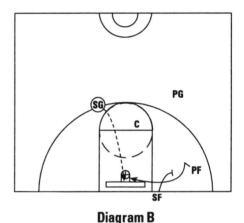

Diagram B

Drill #22: Clear Out For C

Objective: To safely inbound the ball using a box set.

Description: The drill begins with the players positioned as shown in Diagram A. The center (C) cuts to the corner for the inbound pass. The small forward (SF) immediately goes to the lower block and establishes a good post-up position. C attempts to get the ball into SF on the post. If that option is not open, C passes out to the point guard (PG) as the power forward (PF) breaks through the lane looking for the ball. The offside of the floor is now cleared of defenders (Diagram B). PG passes to PF at the foul line, and SF sets a backscreen for C. C v-cuts off the pick into the lane looking for the ball from PF. If C's defender fights through the screen, C should be a step or two ahead. If the defense switches, C has a size advantage over his new defender. Diagram C illustrates another option if C cannot get open underneath. PF swings the ball to the shooting guard (SG) on the offside wing, then move down the lane to set a pick for the SF. SF breaks off the screen to the high post to receive the pass from SG and take the quick jump-shot.

Coaching Point:

- Unless SF is open in the low post after inbounding the ball, this play should focus on clearing out the offside and creating the possible mismatch for C.

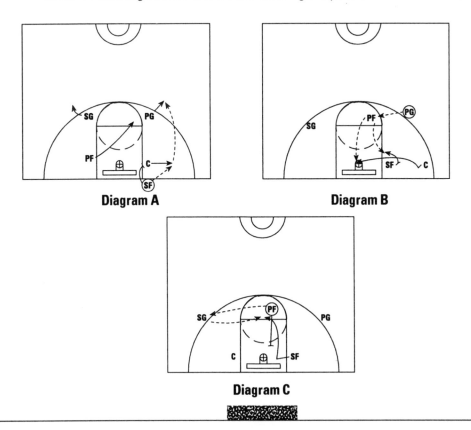

Diagram A   **Diagram B**

Diagram C

Drill #23: Last Gasp Drill

Objective: To safely inbound the ball using a box set; to practice getting a quick, last-second shot against a man-to-man defense.

Description: The drill begins with the players positioned as shown in the diagram below. The point guard (PG) clears to the sideline, and the center (C) breaks toward the basket looking for a lob pass from the shooting guard (SG). The small forward (SF) moves down the lane to set a pick for the power forward (PF). After SF screens, he rolls hard toward the inbounder looking for a pass deep in the lane. PF loops around SF's screen into the lane looking for a pass and the short jump-shot. Meanwhile, PG has been working without the ball to shake his defender. PG serves as the fourth, and least desirable, alternative for the inbound pass since any quick shot he could get would be from long range.

Coaching Point:

- If his team has any time outs available, SG should be instructed to use one if none of the primary options are open.

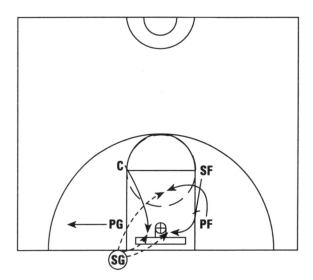

Drill #24: Beat the Trap

Objective: To safely inbound the ball using a box set; to prepare for a team that traps the ball after the inbound pass.

Description: The drill begins with the ball in the shooting guard's (SG) hands and the rest of the offense positioned as shown in the diagram below. The small forward (SF) and center (C) screen their men to the inside to keep them from taking part in a double-team trap. The point guard (PG) v-cuts to get open and breaks to the ballside wing to receive the inbound pass. After inbounding the ball, SG cuts along the baseline to the offside and loops around the screen set by C. PG attempts to find SG with a bounce pass for an open jump-shot. The power forward (PF) has cleared out the side for SG, and is in position at the top of the key to help PG if the cross court pass is not open.

Coaching Point:

- This play is most effective against teams that trap out of a 2-3 zone or man-to-man defense.

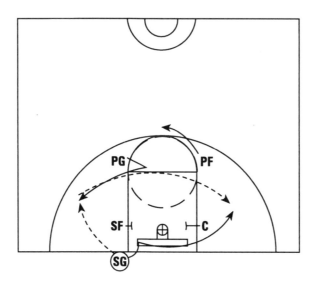

Drill #25: Small Box Lob

Objective: To safely inbound the ball using a box set.

Description: The drill begins with the offense positioned in a closed-up box formation as shown in the diagram below. The shooting guard (SG) is inbounding the ball. The point guard (PG) breaks out of the box to the high wing and serves as a last-choice receiver. The small forward (SF) breaks to the corner, drawing his defender away from the basket. The power forward (PF) screens his defender away from the center (C), and C moves in behind the PF's pick to receive the inbound pass. PG should lob the ball to C down low in the lane.

Coaching Point:

- The necessity of physically moving the screen toward the basket to create a lane for C to penetrate should be emphasized to PF.

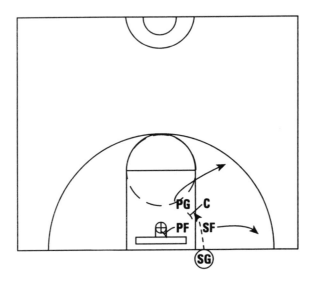

Drill #26: Free the Guards

Objective: To safely inbound the ball using a box set.

Description: The drill begins with the ball in the small forward's (SF) hands and the rest of the offense positioned as shown in the diagram below. The power forward (PF) and center (C) break up the lane to set a double screen for the point guard (PG) and shooting guard (SG). PG and SG execute a crossing maneuver cutting off the barricade provided by the post players. Both guards head toward the ball, giving SF a choice of two players for the inbound pass. After screening, C rolls outside to act as a safety, and PF rolls down the lane toward the ball to offer SF a third option.

Coaching Points:

- The physical nature of the double screen set by the post players should be emphasized.

- PG and SG should set up their respective defenders before cutting off the screen.

- If the defensive guards switch, this play should be run again. This time have PF pick off PG's defender, preventing the switch and allowing SG to scrape his opponent off and come open for the pass.

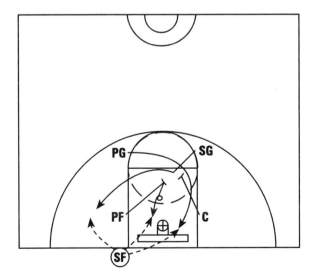

Drill #27: Get Little on Big

Objective: To safely inbound the ball using a box set; to practice forcing the defense into a switching situation to create a size advantage for the offense.

Description: The drill begins with the players positioned as shown in the diagram below. The shooting guard (SG) moves across and down the lane to set a pick for the center (C). The C uses a v-cut to break across the lane for the inbound pass. The small forward (SF) breaks to the sideline to offer the power forward (PF) a second option for the inbound pass. The point guard (PG) crosses to the ballside high wing to offer a safety option in case the two primary receivers are not open.

Coaching Point:

- The importance of setting a solid screen that C's defender cannot fight through should be emphasized to SG. This maneuver forces the switch and the size mismatch to C's advantage.

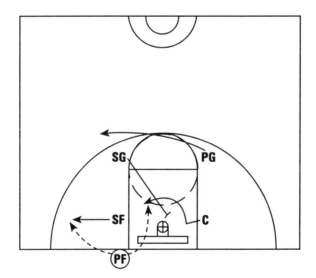

Drill #28: Screen, Double Screen

Objective: To safely inbound the ball using a box set.

Description: This drill begins with the shooting guard (SG) inbounding the ball and the rest of the offense positioned as shown in the diagram below. The small forward (SF) crosses the lane to set a pick for the point guard (PG). PG runs his defender into the pick and breaks to the ballside wing to receive the inbound pass. After PG clears the center of the lane, the power forward (PF) and center (C) move down the lane and set up a barricade on SF's defender. SF loops around the double screen to receive a pass from PG near the top of the key for a jump-shot. PF then posts up on the ballside of the key, and SG moves to the weakside wing to offer SF alternatives if the shot is not open.

Coaching Point:

• Good screens by SF, PF, and C are critical to the success of this play.

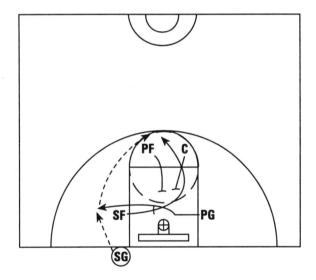

Drill #29: Beat the Zone

Objective: To safely inbound the ball using a box set; to practice a play that is effective against a team that uses a zone on the inbound pass.

Description: This drill begins with the shooting guard (SG) inbounding the ball and the rest of the offense positioned as shown in the diagram below. The point guard (PG) moves toward the center of the key, then v-cuts sharply back to the ballside wing to give SG one inbound option. The center (C) slides in behind the defensive center to set a screen keeping his opponent down low. The power forward (PF) breaks to the center of the lane behind C's screen. SG looks to deliver a lob pass to PF, and the small forward breaks down the lane to the offside low post, providing another option to SG.

Coaching Point:

• The importance of physically moving his defender as far under the basket as possible when setting the screen should be emphasized to C.

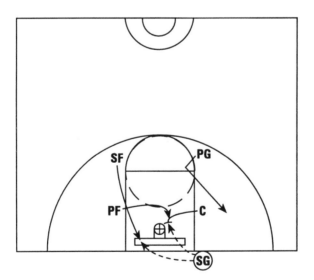

Drill #30: Quadruple Option

Objective: To safely inbound the ball using a box set.

Description: This drill begins with the small forward (SF) inbounding the ball and the rest of the offense positioned as shown in the diagram below. Both post players move up the lane to screen for the guards. The center (C) and shooting guard (SG) are on the ballside; the power forward (PF) and point guard (PG) are on the offside. After setting the screen, C rolls back to the ball. SG breaks to the wide ballside wing. C and SG represent SF's first two options. If the screen is effective, the defense is forced to switch, creating a size advantage for C. After screening for PG, PF rolls back through the lane directly toward the inbounder. PG breaks to the baseline looking for a pass as well.

Coaching Point:

- SG should be patient and wait for C to set a solid pick before breaking to look for the inbound pass and quick shot.

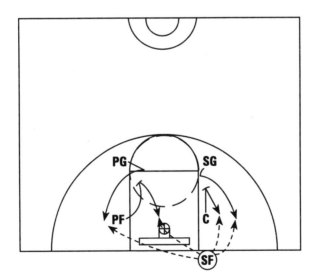

Drill #31: Screen for the Screener

Objective: To safely inbound the ball using a box set; to practice a play that forces the defenders to choose between staying with their man or switching.

Description: This drill begins with the shooting guard (SG) inbounding the ball and the rest of the offense positioned as shown in the diagram below. The center (C) moves up the lane to set a pick for the point guard (PG). PG breaks to the ballside wing looking for the inbound pass, and a shot if it is open. After screening, C receives a screen from the power forward (PF) coming across the lane. C loops around the screen to the basket looking for the inbound pass, and PF rolls back down the lane directly toward the ball. The small forward (SF) remains outside serving as a safe last option.

Coaching Point:

* Setting good, physical screens should be emphasized. Good screens force the defenders to switch, creating favorable mismatches, and have the potential for miscommunication by the defense, giving the offense an advantage.

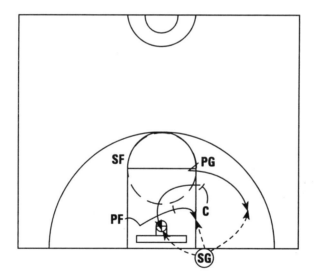

Drill #32: Keep Size On Your Side

Objective: To safely inbound the ball using a box set.

Description: This drill begins with the point guard (PG) inbounding the ball and the rest of the offense positioned as illustrated in the diagram below. The small forward (SF) breaks toward the sideline to take the inbound pass, and PG then moves to the offside wing. The center (C) is the first player to break into the lane looking for a pass from SF. If he is open right away, SF passes into the lane. If C does not receive the pass, he moves on across the lane and sets a backscreen for the shooting guard (SG). SG moves off the pick down the lane toward the basket. SF tries to find SG in the lane with a lob pass. If that is not available, SF passes out to the top of the key to the power forward (PF) who has moved over to serve as an outlet.

Coaching Point:

- The necessity of setting a strong pick on SG's defender should be emphasized to C. If the defense can be forced to switch, a size advantage is created in C's favor.

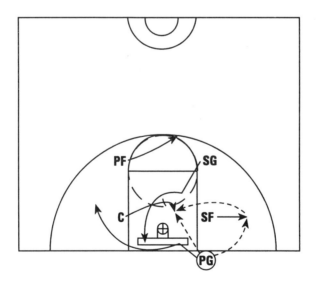

Drill #33: Lob the Zone

Objective: To safely inbound the ball using a box set; to practice a play that is successful against zone defenses.

Description: This drill begins with the players positioned as shown in the diagram below. The power forward (PF) breaks down through the lane to set a backscreen on the middle post defender in the zone. The point guard (PG) and the shooting guard (SG) break to the sidelines to draw their defenders outside. The center (C) then follows PF down the lane looking for the lob pass from the small forward (SF).

Coaching Point:

- This play is very effective against a 2-3 zone, providing PF sets a good screen on the middle post defender. The team should work on setting that screen until any player who might be in that position has mastered the technique.

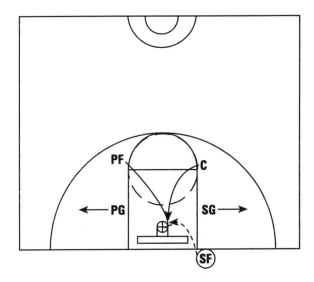

Drill #34: Give a Screen, Get a Screen

Objective: To safely inbound the ball using a box set.

Description: This drill begins with the ball in the shooting guard's (SG) hands and the rest of the offense positioned as shown in the diagram below. The small forward (SF) moves from the offside high wing to the ballside high wing to serve as a last option for SG if none of the three primary targets are open. The point guard (PG) breaks across the lane and sets a pick for the power forward (PF) to cut off of on his way to the basket. After setting the screen for PF, PG receives a pick from the center (C). PG breaks off the pick to the low wing, and C rolls toward the inbounder. This maneuver gives SG three options for the inbound pass, all capable of producing an open shot.

Coaching Point:

- If PG screens well enough for PF to force a switch by the defense, PF will have a distinct size advantage over PG's defender.

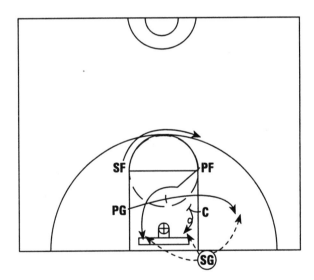

Drill #35: Get the Ball in Low

Objective: To safely inbound the ball using a box set.

Description: This play begins with the small forward (SF) inbounding the ball and the rest of the offense positioned as shown in the diagram below. The shooting guard (SG) slides out high to serve as a safety valve. The center (C) moves diagonally up the lane to set a pick for the point guard (PG). PG cuts off the screen to the ballside wing looking for the inbound pass. The power forward (PF) moves over and sets a screen on C's defender. C breaks around the pick to the basket, and PF rolls back toward the inbounder. If the defense switches, PF should be open on the reverse pivot. If the defenders stay man-to-man, C should have a one- or two-step advantage on his defender coming off the screen.

Coaching Point:

- The more a team screens, the better the chance of defensive mis-communication, which works in the offense's favor.

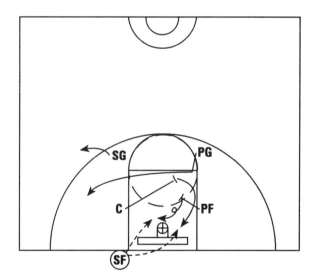

CHAPTER 2

STACK SETS

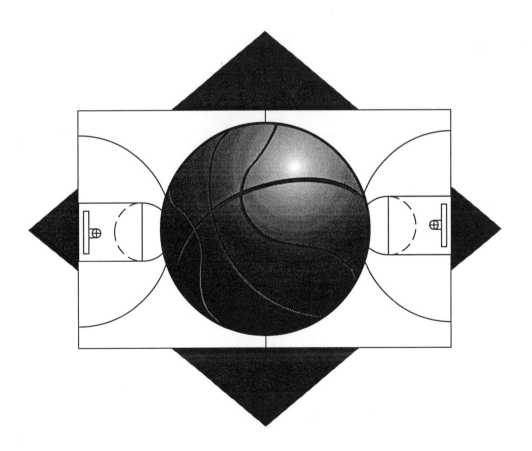

Drill #36: Around the Horn to the Backdoor

Objective: To safely inbound the ball using a stack set.

Description: The drill begins with the ball in the point guard's (PG) hands and the rest of the offense positioned as shown in Diagram A. The small forward (SF) moves down the lane to screen for the center (C). C breaks off the pick to the outside wing. The power forward (PF) crosses the lane diagonally to the ballside wing. This maneuver clears the offside of the floor. The shooting guard (SG) breaks out to take the inbound pass, and PG moves to the offside low wing. SG starts the ball around the horn to PF, who passes to C. Meanwhile, PG has been attempting to get his defender to overplay to open up the backdoor opportunity. If the defender is too aggressive, the backdoor should be there. If the defender is playing soft, C passes down to PG on the wing (Diagram B). SF sets a screen for PF, who breaks down the lane. SF cuts off a pick from C to the top of the key. PG either finds PF in the lane or goes to SF for the jump-shot.

Coaching Points:

- The importance of breaking hard to the wing after the inbound pass to attempt to get the chasing defender out of control should be emphasized.

- Rapid ball movement around the perimeter should also be stressed.

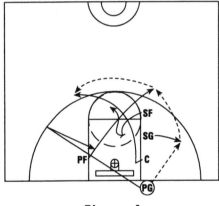

Diagram A

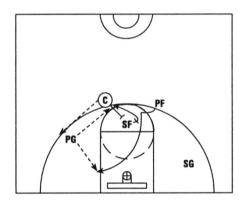

Diagram B

Drill #37: Quick Shot for SG

Objective: To safely inbound the ball using a stack set.

Description: This drill begins with the small forward (SF) inbounding the ball and the rest of the offense positioned as shown in Diagram A. The point guard (PG) breaks to the corner looking for the inbound pass. The center (C) breaks out of the stack in front of the basket and attempts to get position on the defender to receive a pass. The power forward (PF) moves from the top of the stack to the bottom, also alert for a pass. The shooting guard (SG), in the offside corner, is SF's primary target. If SF can get the ball to SG, a quick shot by the team's best shooter will follow. If not, PG takes the inbound pass and looks to PF, who establishes a post-up position on his defender (Diagram B). C moves down to screen for SF, who breaks off the screen to the foul line looking for the pass from PG and the jump-shot.

Coaching Point:

- It should be emphasized to SG that he should be even with the backboard in the offside corner to give SF a good angle for the pass.

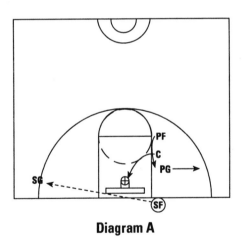

Diagram A

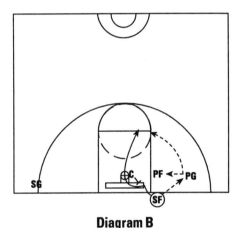

Diagram B

Drill #38: Horizontal Stack

Objective: To safely inbound the ball using a stack set.

Description: This drill begins with the point guard (PG) inbounding the ball and the rest of the offense stacked as shown in Diagram A. The power forward (PF) and center (C) break down through the lane and execute a crossing maneuver in an attempt to make their defenders switch. The shooting guard (SG) and small forward (SF) break to the wings, and PG inbounds the ball to SG. PG then cuts up the lane to the ballside top of the key. If PF and C are successful in forcing the switch, SG checks to see if either is open for a lob. If not, SG passes back to PG, and phase two of the play begins (Diagram B). PF sets a pick for SF on the offside wing and then breaks toward PG. SF breaks into the lane looking to PG for the pass. If it is not open, SF sets a pick for C, who breaks up the lane directly toward PG creating another option. Diagram C illustrates further options. If PF receives a pass from PG and cannot shoot, SF moves on through the lane off a pick from SG to spring free on the wing. C then screens for SG and rolls back toward PF. SG breaks to the opposite wing for a pass and the jump-shot.

Coaching Point:

- Repetition is the key to developing the necessary flow from one option to the next.

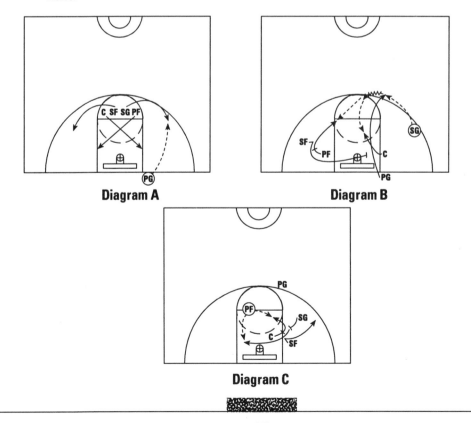

Diagram A

Diagram B

Diagram C

Drill #39: Inbound For Three

Objective: To safely inbound the ball using a stack set; to set up a team's best shooter for a quick three-point shot.

Description: This drill begins with the ball in the small forward's (SF) hands and the rest of the offensive players stacked as shown in Diagram A. The point guard (PG) sets a screen on the shooting guard's (SG) defender. The screen is set to the inside to make SG's defender think he is going to the lane. SG fakes to the lane and v-cuts sharply back to the ballside wing to take the inbound pass and three-point shot. If the shot is not open, the center (C) and power forward (PF) form a double screen for SG along the lane line. SG passes out to PG in front and breaks into the lane, attempting to get his defender behind the wall set up by the post players. SG then cuts sharply back out to the three-point line looking for the pass from PG and the shot (Diagram B). After inbounding the ball, SF moves to the offside wing and remains there as an outlet for PG if SG cannot shake free.

Coaching Point:

• The importance of good fakes to set up his cuts to the three-point line should be emphasized.

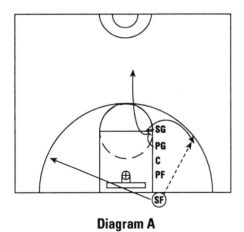

Diagram A

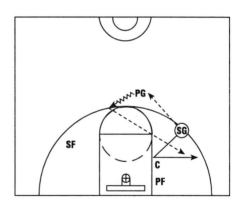

Diagram B

Drill #40: Two-Player Game

Objective: To safely inbound the ball using a stack set.

Description: This drill begins with the ball in the small forward's (SF) hands and the rest of the offense positioned as shown in Diagram A. The power forward (PF) breaks into the lane under the basket and attempts to secure position to receive the inbound pass. The point guard (PG) breaks hard to the corner, and the center (C) cuts down the lane line looking for the pass. The shooting guard (SG) is in the offside corner. All four are considered primary options for SF unless designated otherwise by the coach. It is usually PG who is the most wide open. If PG gets the ball, he and C are in perfect position to execute an inside-outside two-player game.

Coaching Points:

- The necessity of establishing good position in the lane with physical play should be emphasized to PF and C.

- SG should be even with the backboard to create a good passing angle for SF.

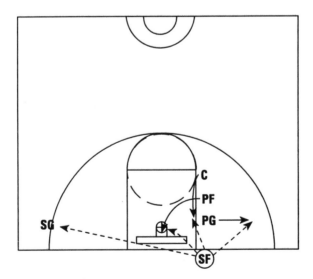

Drill #41: The Blockade

Objective: To safely inbound the ball using a stack set.

Description: The drill begins with the players positioned as illustrated in Diagram A. The power forward (PF) and center (C) break across the lane and maneuver to set up a double screen. The shooting guard (SG) fakes as if to head across the lane with the post players, then cuts back out to the ballside wing to take the inbound pass. After inbounding, the small forward (SF) moves along the baseline around the double screen to the weakside wing. On receiving the inbound pass, SG passes to the point guard (PG), who dribbles into position to hit SF on the wing as he cuts around the double screen. If SF cannot get a good shot, the ball is passed back out to PG. PF rolls quickly off the double screen directly toward PG to take a pass at the foul line. Meanwhile, C works under the basket to get position on his defender to be open for a lob pass from PF (Diagram B).

Coaching Point:

- The double screen by PF and C should be close enough to the baseline that SF can get by, but so close there is no room for his defender to avoid the blockade.

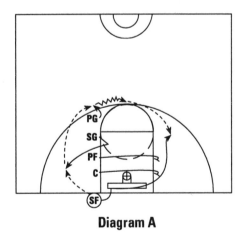

Diagram A

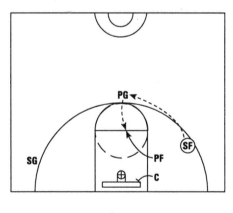

Diagram B

Drill #42: Clear Out the Baseline

Objective: To safely inbound the ball using a stack set.

Description: This drill begins with the small forward (SF) attempting to inbound the ball and the rest of the offensive players in a horizontal stack along the foul line as illustrated in the diagram below. The center (C) and power forward (PF) break down the lane to get in position to receive the inbound pass and take a short shot. PF, on the ballside, is SF's first choice because it is a shorter pass. In the event of a missed shot, both big players are in the lane in good rebounding position. The shooting guard (SG) and the point guard (PG) also break down the lane before flaring out toward the sidelines. SG is most likely to be open if SF is unable to get the ball in to either post player. PG crosses in front of C going down the lane, and should attempt to hinder C's defender in the process.

Coaching Point:

- The horizontal stack forces the defenders to move off the baseline, clearing the way for PF and C to move toward the basket.

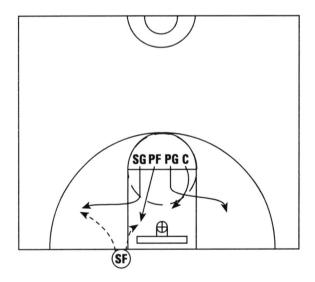

Drill #43: Jump-Shots Off the Stack

Objective: To safely inbound the ball using a stack; to create opportunities for outside jump-shooters.

Description: This drill begins with the small forward (SF) inbounding the ball and the rest of the offensive players stacked along the lane line as shown in Diagram A. The center (C) breaks across the lane to the offside low post, and the shooting guard (SG) moves down to the ballside low post. The power forward (PF) cuts to the sideline for the inbound pass and immediately passes out to the point guard. PF then sets a screen for the inbounder, and SF cuts off the screen to the wing. C crosses the lane to set a pick for G, who cuts off it to the opposite wing. C rolls off the pick directly toward PG (Diagram B). PG can hit either SF or SG for the jumper, or pass into C at the foul line. If C does not get the pass, he moves back to the low post, setting up the alignment illustrated in Diagram C. This maneuver allows PG to take his defender one-on-one and penetrate down the lane for a shot or a pass to either post player.

Coaching Point:

• The primary option on this play is to spring SF or SG free for an open jumper by using good screens by the big players.

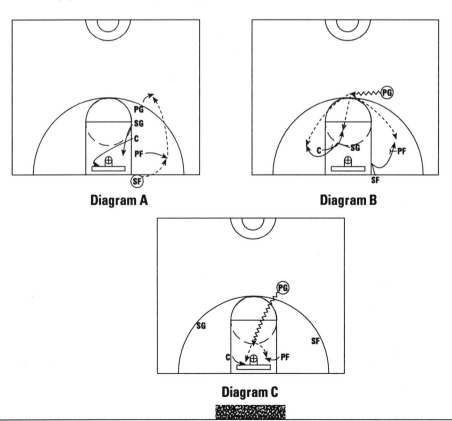

Diagram A   **Diagram B**

Diagram C

Drill #44: PG's Play

Objective: To safely inbound the ball using a stack set.

Description: This drill begins with the point guard (PG) inbounding the ball and the rest of the offensive players in a horizontal stack along the foul line as illustrated in the diagram below. The power forward (PF) and the small forward (SF) set a solid double screen at the foul line to keep defenders to the inside. The shooting guard (SG) breaks out of the stack to the wing to take the inbound pass. SG dribbles across the top of the key as PG breaks up the lane. C moves down the lane and establishes a screen allowing PG to cut back to the wing, scraping his defender off in the process. After screening, C establishes a good post-up position down low. SG feeds PG the ball on the wing, and PG shoots if the shot is open. If not, PG starts a two-player game with C.

Coaching Point:

- SG must time his dribble across the top of the key to be at the proper passing angle when PG pops open on the wing.

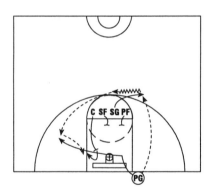

Drill #45: Delay and Break

Objective: To safely inbound the ball using a stack set.

Description: This drill begins with the point guard inbounding the ball and the rest of the offensive players stacked along the lane line as illustrated in Diagram A. The shooting guard (SG) is stationed at the offside low post. The small forward (SF), power forward (PF), and center (C) stay in place, executing head fakes and misdirection steps until the SG has time to break diagonally up the lane and set a screen for C. As C cuts off the screen toward the basket, PF breaks down the lane to the inbounder. SF breaks hard to the corner to serve as an outlet for PG if C and PF cannot get open. When SF catches the inbound pass, PG moves in to screen for PF, allowing him to establish a good post position. After screening, PG breaks to the offside wing around a screen set by C in the lane. SF now has three options, as shown in Diagram B. He can pass into the post to PF, find PG cross court, or pass outside to SG if nothing else is open.

Coaching Point:

- The timing of the original break from the stack by SF, PF, and C is critical. They need to move as one entity to make the play effective.

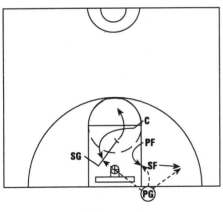

Diagram A

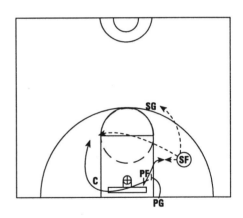

Diagram B

Drill #46: "Pulling Guard" Drill

Objective: To safely inbound the ball using a stack set.

Description: The drill begins with the players stacked along the lane line as illustrated in Diagram A and the small forward (SF) inbounding the ball. All four players in the stack move simultaneously. The point guard (PG) shifts out high to provide an emergency outlet for SF. The shooting guard (SG) fakes into the lane and cuts to the corner to serve as the second option on the play. The center (C) acts like the pulling guard leading a sweep and crashes into the lane, taking anyone in front of him along for the ride. The power forward (PF) follows behind C to move down the lane for a lob pass. If SF has to settle for getting the ball to SG, he fakes up the lane and moves around the baseline side of a low screen set by C. SG passes out to PG at the high wing, and SF cuts off C's pick up the lane looking for a pass from PG and a jumper.

Coaching Point:

- C needs to run interference as if merely fighting through traffic to avoid getting called for a foul or a moving screen.

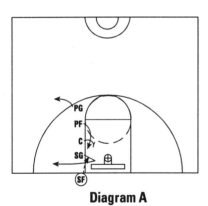

Diagram A

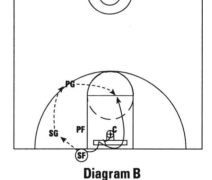

Diagram B

Drill #47: Two Options, Then a Triangle

Objective: To safely inbound the ball using a stack set.

Description: This drill begins with the point guard (PG) attempting to inbound the ball and rest of the offense positioned as shown in Diagram A. The small forward (SF), the first player to break out of the stack, cuts to the sideline to take the quick inbound pass from PG. As the pass is made, the power forward (PF) breaks diagonally down the lane to set a pick for the shooting guard (SG), who cuts off the screen back up the lane looking for a pass from SF and the jumper. As soon as SG has broken off the screen, PF breaks back toward the ball, giving SF two options. If neither player is open, the players form a triangle as illustrated in Diagram B. SF can either feed the center (C) in the post to start a two-player game, or give SG time to work open outside and pass the ball out. If SG gets the ball, PF should break directly up the lane toward the ball as C attempts to get inside position on his defender. When PF gets the ball, a shot is taken if it is open, or PF can go inside to C if he has successfully established inside position.

Coaching Point:

- If C is unable to seal off his defender, he should move out to set a pick for SF, who cuts to the lane looking for a pass from PF.

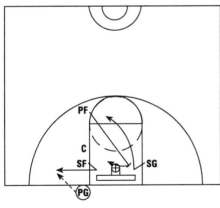

Diagram A

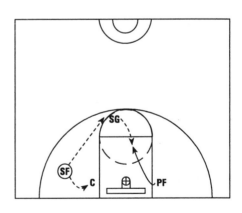

Diagram B

Drill #48: The Squeeze Screen

Objective: To safely inbound the ball using a stack set.

Description: This drill begins with the shooting guard (SG) inbounding the ball and the rest of the offensive players stacked along the lane line as shown in the diagram below. The center (C) and small forward (SF) set a double-team "squeeze" screen to keep the power forward's (PF) defender from following him as he breaks to the wing. As PF clears to the wing, the point guard (PG) cuts around the double screen in an attempt to interfere with any defender chasing PF outside. PG then clears out to the opposite side of the floor. SG gets the inbound pass in to PF for the quick jump-shot.

Coaching Points:

- The double screen must be quick and tough.

- The timing of PG's move around the screen behind PF's break is critical.

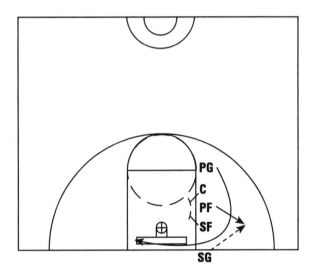

Drill #49: Scatter Drill

Objective: To safely inbound the ball using a modified stack set.

Description: This drill begins with the shooting guard (SG) inbounding the ball and the rest of the offense positioned as shown in the diagram below. Notice that the small forward (SF) is positioned just behind the power forward (PF), who is in the middle of a horizontal three-player stack. This maneuver is a simple and effective play that gives SG four options. The point guard (PG) breaks to the wing while SF and PF break down to their respective blocks. The center (C) swings out to offer a choice over the top of the defense. If the inbounder realizes that SF's defender is not in the area, he can signal to PG, PF, and C to hold the line and screen down. SG then passes over the top of the defense to SF.

Coaching Points:

- Quickness is the key to getting open on this play.

- The cutters must be ready to move on a given signal from the inbounder.

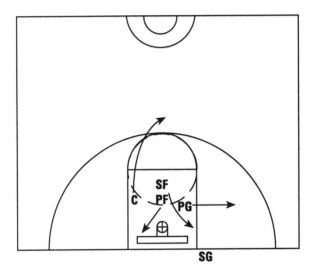

CHAPTER 3

DIAMOND SETS

Drill #50: C's Play

Objective: To safely inbound the ball using a diamond set; to attempt to get a quick score by the center.

Description: This play begins with the point guard (PG) inbounding the ball and the rest of the players positioned as illustrated in the diagram below. The shooting guard (SG) slides to the outside to serve as a final option and a safety. The center (C) breaks diagonally up the lane and sets a screen for the small forward (SF) at the foul line. SF breaks off the screen to the ballside wing and serves as PG's second choice for an inbound target. The power forward (PF) moves across the lane and sets the key screen for C. C rolls off his screen, cuts around the screen by PF, and breaks directly to the basket. PG gets the ball to C for the easy basket, and goes to SF or SG only if C is not open.

Coaching Points:

- PF should be on his way to the lane as C is setting the first screen.

- The screens need to be set in quick succession to be effective.

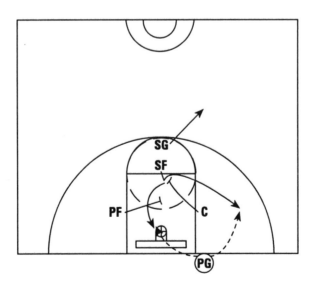

Drill #51: Inside First, Outside Second

Objective: To safely inbound the ball using a diamond set.

Description: This drill begins with the players positioned as illustrated in Diagram A. The small forward (SF) cuts to the corner to clear out the low post. The center (C) moves quickly across the lane looking for the inbound pass. The power forward (PF) fakes as if to join the action on the ball side and v-cuts to the low post position vacated by C. The shooting guard's (SG) first option is to look to the big players down low. Meanwhile, the point guard (PG) moves outside and becomes SG's second choice for the inbound pass. As the pass is made, C posts up in the lane looking for the pass from PG, and SG moves to the offside wing behind a pick from PF (Diagram B). PG may hit SG coming off the screen, or find C, who can either turn for the jumper or deliver the ball to SG. The third choice is shown in Diagram C. SG passes to SF in the corner. As the pass is made, C moves across the lane and sets a pick for the inbounder. SG loops around the screen looking for the return pass from SF and slips into the lane for a jumper.

Coaching Point:

- The inbounder should look specifically to the three options in the order listed above.

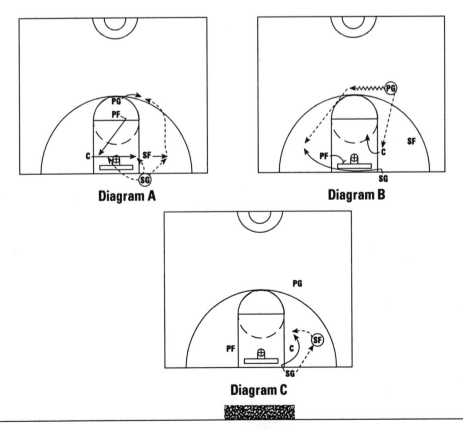

Diagram A

Diagram B

Diagram C

Drill #52: Multiple Choice

Objective: To safely inbound the ball using a diamond set.

Description: This drill begins with the point guard (PG) inbounding the ball and the rest of the offense positioned as shown in Diagram A. The center (C) and small forward (SF) move diagonally through the lane to set a double screen for the shooting guard (SG). The power forward (PF) breaks sharply to the sideline to take the inbound pass, and SG cuts off the double screen to the top of the key for a pass from PF. SG should be open for the jump-shot unless the defense switches out of the double screen. In that case, SF should flash back through the lane for the ball and a quick jumper. Further choices are illustrated in Diagram B. The ball is passed from PG to PF to SG on top. Then C and SF move down and set a second double screen for PG. PG breaks along the baseline around the screen to the wing for a pass from SG and a jump-shot. In another option, SF sets a third screen on the play for C. C cuts around the pick and goes up the lane to get a pass from SG for the turn-around jumper.

Coaching Point:

* Practice the many options of this drill so the players are comfortable with all of them.

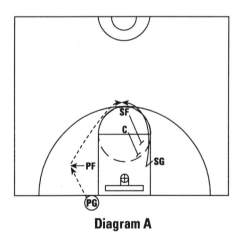

Diagram A

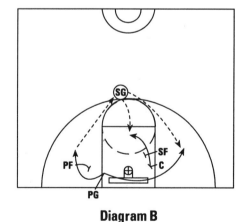

Diagram B

Drill #53: Diamond to C

Objective: To safely inbound the ball using a diamond set.

Description: This drill begins with the players positioned as illustrated in the diagram below. The center (C) is the primary target for the inbound pass, and his height should make that a safe option. After inbounding the ball, the power forward (PF) establishes a good low post-up position on his defender. The point guard (PG) and the shooting guard (SG) move diagonally down the lane and set a double screen for the small forward (SF). SF breaks around the screen to the top of the key. This gives C two places to go with the ball. He may hit SF for the jump-shot, or feed the ball to PF on the low post.

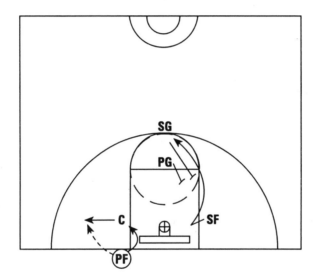

CHAPTER 4

BASELINE SETS

Drill #54: Use the Advantage

Objective: To safely inbound the ball using a baseline set.

Description: This play begins with the shooting guard (SG) inbounding the ball and the rest of the offensive players positioned as illustrated in Diagram A. The center (C) breaks back to the edge of the foul line and receives the inbound pass from SG over the top of the defense. As the pass is made, the power forward (PF) breaks up to the opposite edge of the foul line, clearing out that side of the lane in the process. SG steps inbounds and sets a screen for the small forward (Diagram B). SF breaks off the screen into the lane, and SG rolls back toward PF, who has received a pass from C. PF can find either SF or SG in the lane for a quick jump-shot over the defense.

Coaching Point:

- This play is particularly advantageous when either SG or SF has a height advantage on his defender.

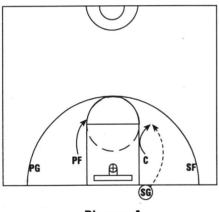

Diagram A

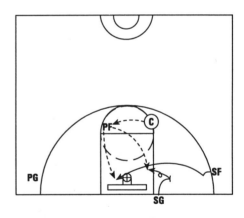

Diagram B

Drill #55: Two Screens for SF

Objective: To safely inbound the ball using a baseline set.

Description: This drill begins with the shooting guard (SG) inbounding the ball and the rest of the offensive players positioned as shown in the diagram below. The power forward (PF) sets a screen for the small forward (SF), who breaks across the lane. The center (C) sets a second pick for SF near the middle of the lane, and SF runs his defender into the pick and cuts sharply toward the baseline. After screening, both C and PF roll toward the basket looking for the lob pass. SG's first priority is to get the ball to SF for the lay-up if he springs free off the two screens. If no one is open inside, SG goes over the top to PG, who has moved outside to act as a safety.

Coaching Point:

- A second option involves having PF screen for SF if SF's defender tries to stay with him by moving along the baseline. After screening, PF should attempt to seal his defender.

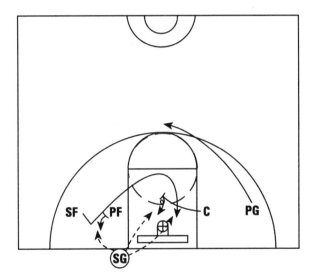

Drill #56: Baseline Triple Option

Objective: To safely inbound the ball using a baseline set.

Description: This drill begins with the players positioned as illustrated in Diagram A. The shooting guard (SG) breaks to the ballside top of the key, and the power forward (PF) fills the vacated spot in the corner. The small forward (SF) inbounds the ball to PF and fakes a move up the lane. He then loops around a double screen from the center (C) and point guard (PG) back into the lane. PF's first option is to find SF in the lane for a jumper. In the second option (Diagram B), SF cuts off the double screen and continues to the wing. After screening, C breaks across the lane toward the ball looking for the inside pass from PF. PF may also reverse the ball to SG at the ballside top of the key. PG leaves the screen and breaks to the offside top of the key to receive a pass from SG. SF observes the defense and either loops around C's screen to the lane or continues to the wing as the defense dictates. PG finds SF in either place with the pass. Diagram C illustrates this completion of the baseline triple option.

Coaching Point:

- In the first option, the coach should stress to PG the need to move quickly to set up the double screen with C.

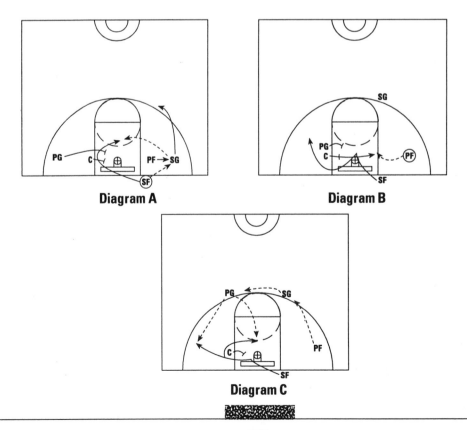

Diagram A   Diagram B

Diagram C

Drill #57: Set Up the Shooter

Objective: To safely inbound the ball using a baseline set.

Description: This drill begins with the players positioned along the baseline as shown in Diagram A and the point guard (PG) inbounding the ball. The small forward (SF) sprints to the ballside top of the key and the shooting guard (SG) cuts behind SF to the basket. The power forward (PF) sets a pick for the center (C), who cuts around it to the lane. If either inside pass is open, PG delivers the ball, cutting short the designed play. If not, PF breaks to the sideline for the inbound pass. SF moves down from the top of the key to set a screen for C and continues to the offside low post vacated by SG. C breaks off SF's pick to the top of the key to take the pass from PF (Diagram B). After inbounding, PG moves to the ballside low post and receives a screen from PF. PG pops out from the baseline side of the screen to receive a pass from C for the outside shot (Diagram C).

Coaching Point:

- This play is designed for the best shooter on your team. That player should inbound the ball.

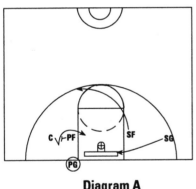

Diagram A

Diagram B

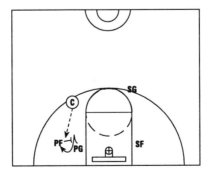

Diagram C

CHAPTER 5

RANDOM
SETS

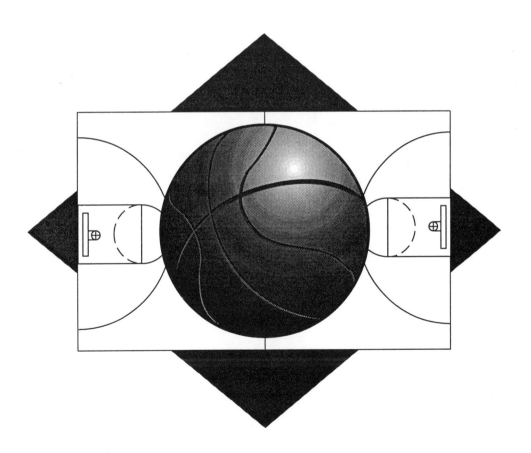

Drill #58: Read the Screen

Objective: To safely inbound the ball using a random set.

Description: This drill begins with the shooting guard (SG) inbounding the ball and the rest of the offense positioned as illustrated in Diagram A. The small forward (SF) remains outside as a safety valve in both options. The center (C) screens for the point guard (PG). PG moves strongly to the baseline, reverses direction, and cuts off the pick to the wing for the inbound pass and jumper. If the shot is not open, PG has two remaining options. The power forward (PF) moves to the offside edge of the foul line to set a screen for the inbounder. SG loops around the screen to the top of the key. PG may either hit SG for the jump-shot or begin a two player game with C. A second option is to give PG the choice of reading the screen set by C. If PG cuts off the screen in the direction opposite his defender, it might force a switch. This creates a mismatch and C opens up to the ball looking for the pass (Diagram B).

Coaching Point:

- If PG can force the switch, the second option is preferable.

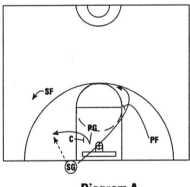

Diagram A

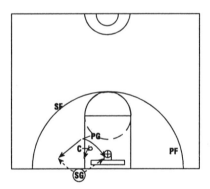

Diagram B

Drill #59: Backscreen and Lob

Objective: To safely inbound the ball using a random set.

Description: This drill begins with the ball in the small forward's (SF) hands and the rest of the offensive players positioned as shown in Diagram A. The center (C) moves toward the lane and veers out to receive the inbound pass. C immediately passes out to the point guard (PG), and PG dribbles to the opposite side of the floor. The power forward (PF) sets a backscreen on the shooting guard's (SG) defender. SG breaks around the screen toward the basket looking for a lob from PG. PG can also continue to move toward PF as he sets the screen. This maneuver alerts PF to break off that screen and move over to set a screen with C for the inbounder. SF breaks around the screen to the edge of the foul line. PG can decide whether SF or SG has the more open shot.

Coaching Point:

- Rapid ball reversal from C to PG and a good screen from PF are critical.

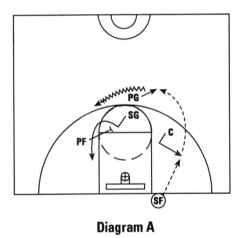

Diagram A

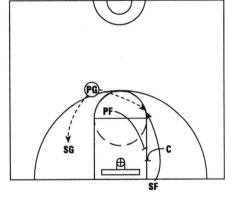

Diagram B

Drill #60: Spread 'Em Outside

Objective: To safely inbound the ball using a random set; to keep the play off the baseline to allow room to maneuver.

Description: This drill begins with the shooting guard (SG) inbounding the ball and the rest of the offense positioned as illustrated in Diagram A. The power forward (PF) and the center (C) move inside to set screens for the small forward (SF) and the point guard (PG). SF and PG must both read the defense, react accordingly, and cut hard to the ball. C and PF both roll to the outside off their picks. This maneuver gives SG four options for the pass.

Coaching Point:

- Starting the offensive players in a far outside position gives them all a chance to receive the inbound pass and have room to maneuver one-on-one.

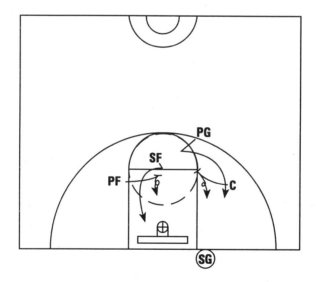

Drill #61: PG's Choice

Objective: To safely inbound the ball using a random set.

Description: The drill begins with the players positioned as illustrated in the diagram below. The point guard (PG) gets into position to receive a pass from the shooting guard (SG), who has cut to the corner to take the inbound pass. The small forward (SF) streaks toward the power forward (PF) on the far side of the lane. If SF's defender gets out of control trying to keep up, SF stops short and stays low behind the center (C) for a pass from PG and the easy jumper. If not, SF continues on and stacks up with PF at the edge of the lane. SG clears to the opposite wing around a screen set by C, PF, and SF. PG now has two more options available. He can dribble toward SG and pass to either SG or SF, who has broken off his screen and has come up the lane toward the ball. PG can also dribble back to the spot vacated by SG. From there, PG can pass into C on the post and start a two-player game.

Coaching Point:

- This maneuver is a good play if PG is a sound player physically and mentally.

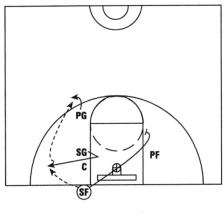

Diagram A

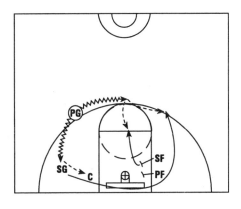

Diagram B

Drill #62: Be Quick Inside

Objective: To safely inbound the ball using a random set.

Description: This drill begins with the small forward (SF) inbounding the ball and the rest of the offensive players positioned as illustrated in Diagram A. The center (C) breaks hard across the lane looking for a lob from SF. The power forward (PF) screens in for the shooting guard (SG) and rolls off the screen to the outside. SG breaks off the screen to receive the inbound pass in case the lob to C was not open. If SG gets the pass, he immediately passes out to PF, who passes on to the point guard (PG) on the opposite side of the floor. At this point, the focus shifts to the inbounder. Both C and SG set screens for SF, who has two options. He must read the defense and come off either side of the screens. Depending on the decision, PG finds SF either in the lane or outside the lane for a jumper (Diagram B).

Coaching Point:

* The quickness and agility of SF inside are critical to the success of this play.

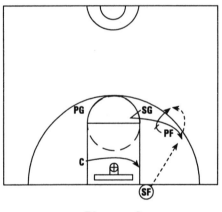

Diagram A

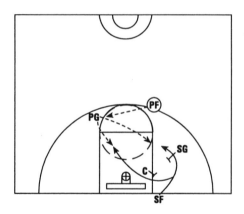

Diagram B

Drill #63: Three Chances For a Quick Score

Objective: To safely inbound the ball using a random set.

Description: This drill begins with the shooting guard (SG) inbounding the ball and the other offensive players positioned as illustrated in the diagram below. The center (C) moves into the lane to screen for the small forward (SF). SF breaks off the screen to the wing, looking for the inbound pass and a quick jump-shot. C rolls off that screen and moves up the lane to set a second pick for the point guard (PG), who breaks off the screen down the lane looking for a pass for the quick score. As C rolls away from his first screen, the power forward (PF) breaks straight down the lane line off of SF's cut looking for the inbound pass and a quick shot.

Coaching Point:

- The timing of PF's break down the line should be practiced. SG should pass immediately after SF moves out to the wing. This action has the effect of using SF for a moving screen.

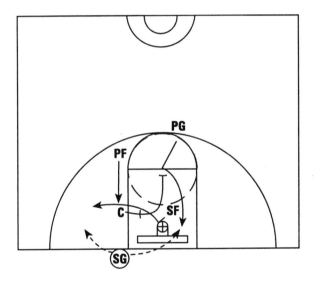

Drill #64: Fill the Vacated Post

Objective: To safely inbound the ball using a random set.

Description: This drill begins with the players positioned as shown in Diagram A. The power forward (PF) and center (C) move quickly in opposite directions. PF breaks to the wing for the inbound pass, and C moves into the lane to post up. The small forward (SF) breaks down the lane line and fills the spot vacated by PF and C. The point guard's (PG) first choice is to find SF free for the easy basket. If not, PG passes to PF on the wing. The shooting guard (SG) has rotated over to the ballside to function as a last chance outlet and a safety. If the ball is inbounded to PF, he immediately passes out to SG (Diagram B). PF then screens for SF, who pops off the pick to the wing. Meanwhile, C has screened for the inbounder, and PG loops around the screen to the lane. SG passes to the most open player for the jumper.

Coaching Point:

- The timing of SF's move to the spot vacated by C and PF should be practiced. If SF arrives quickly enough, there will be enough traffic to slow down his defender.

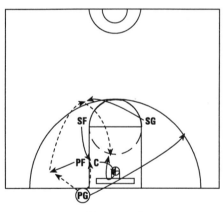

Diagram A

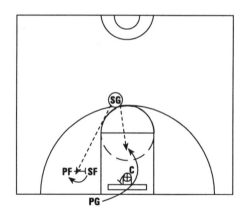

Diagram B

Drill #65: Three Ducks In a Row

Objective: To safely inbound the ball using a random set.

Description: This drill begins with the small forward (SF) inbounding the ball and the other offensive players positioned as illustrated in Diagram A. The power forward (PF) breaks to the sideline for the inbound pass. The center (C) moves in the opposite direction, attempting to gain position to get a lob from the inbounder. If that is open, the pass is made and the play is cut short. The shooting guard (SG) breaks down the lane line to the spot vacated by PF and C. If SG is open, the ball goes there. If not, SF puts the ball in play to PF on the sideline. When the ball is inbounded to PF, SG moves back up the lane line and SF posts up low. PF passes the ball out to the point guard (PG), who dribbles to the opposite side of the floor. While PG is moving cross court, C screens for SF, who breaks around the baseline side of the pick to the wing (Diagram B). C rolls off the screen and sets up in the lane and PF cuts off a pick from SG into the lane. This maneuver gives PG three options: SF on the far right, C in the lane, and PF on the left entering the lane. PG should scan the court from right to left and pass to the best receiver.

Coaching Point:

- The timing of SG's arrival to the spot vacated by PF and C is critical.

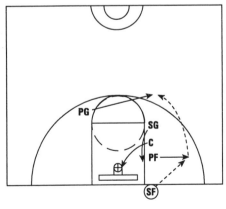

Diagram A

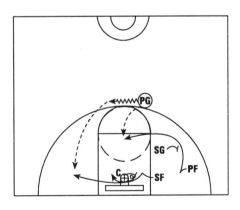

Diagram B

Drill #66: Man-to-Man Special

Objective: To safely inbound the ball using a random set; to practice a play that is effective against an aggressive man-to-man defense.

Description: This drill begins with the players positioned as illustrated in Diagram A. The point guard (PG) moves up the lane and sets a pick for the center (C), who cuts directly down the lane looking for the inbound pass and a quick score. After screening, PG breaks out to the wing behind a double screen from the shooting guard (SG) and the power forward (PF). After screening, SG moves outside to act as a safety. PF rolls to the basket to serve as one of the inbounder's two remaining options. The small forward (SF) passes either to PG on the wing for the jump-shot, or down inside to PF. Diagram B shows a different approach from the same set. PF moves up to screen for SG, who cuts off the screen to the corner for the jumper. After screening, PF rolls down the lane toward the ball. In this variation, PG continues on to the perimeter after screening for C to function as the last inbound option and safety.

Coaching Point:

- Screens against an aggressive man-to-man defense are a good way to get a step ahead of the defender who has to fight through or around the screen.

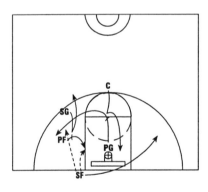

Diagram A

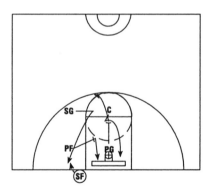

Diagram B

Drill #67: Two Ways to Go For SG

Objective: To safely inbound the ball using a random set.

Description: This drill begins with the shooting guard (SG) inbounding the ball and the other players positioned as illustrated in Diagram A. The ball is inbounded to the point guard (PG), who breaks to the wing off a screen set by the center (C). PG immediately reverses the ball to the small forward (SF) outside. The power forward (PF) moves in to set a screen for SG on the offside of the lane, and C and PG set a double screen for SG on the ballside of the lane. SG must read the defense and react accordingly. He breaks as if coming up the lane, and cuts sharply to take advantage of either screen (Diagram B). SF finds SG on one of the wings for the jumper. For another option, the coach has PG hold the ball. This time, C continues across the lane and sets a second screen for PF (Diagram C). If PF breaks cleanly off the pick, PG passes into the lane immediately. If PF has trouble breaking clean, the ball is reversed to SF, and C attempts to set a second screen for PF. If PF clears this screen, SF delivers the ball.

Coaching Point:

- This play is an excellent way to get the ball in the best shooter's hands. The coach should adjust his personnel so his best shooter is inbounding the ball.

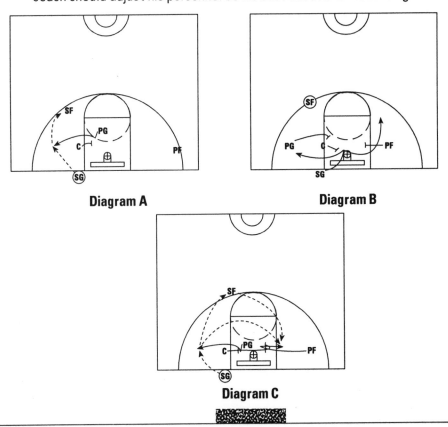

Diagram A

Diagram B

Diagram C

Drill #68: Clear the Lane

Objective: To safely inbound the ball using a random set; to practice plays that clear out the lane and give the big players room to work inside.

Description: The players are positioned as shown in Diagram A. The center (C) sets a pick in the lane for the power forward (PF). PF cuts into the lane for a pass and C rolls back toward the ball. The shooting guard (SG) sets a screen for the point guard (PG), who breaks to the corner. SG rolls back toward the ball. The small forward (SF) then has four inbound options. In Diagram B, PF sets up his defender by breaking high, then maneuvers to gain inside position for the inbound pass. C moves up, then curls back into the lane, pinning his defender inside toward the baseline. PG and SG use the same maneuvers as in the first option. SF looks to PF and C. If SF chooses C, he passes over the top and moves inside for a return pass. In Diagram C, SG clears to the top to act as a safety. PG sets a pick for PF, then moves to the offside wing to clear the post area. PF breaks around the screen into the lane for the lob, and C breaks to the corner. C is most likely to be open. If so, SF posts up low for the feed and a two-player game. Diagram D shows another option. PF maneuvers to receive the inbound pass and C breaks to the sideline to do the same. PG breaks down the side of the lane to receive a short pass. SF takes his pick of the three pass receivers.

Coaching Points:

- All the drills from this set require players to read the defense and react accordingly.

- The return pass from C to SF in Diagram B should be a touch pass in the air, which requires considerable practice.

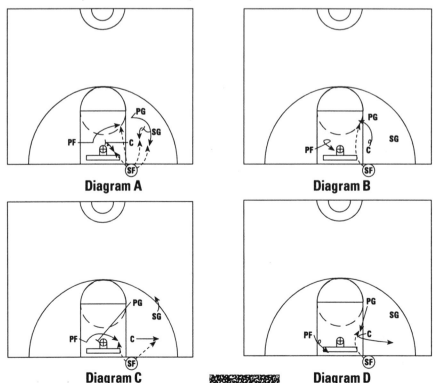

Diagram A   Diagram B

Diagram C   Diagram D

Drill #69: Think Big

Objective: To safely inbound the ball using a random set; to practice a play that will clear the lane and give the post players a chance to maneuver.

Description: This drill begins with the offensive players positioned as shown in Diagram A. The power forward (PF) breaks to the sideline for the pass, and the small forward (SF) quickly inbounds the ball. PF passes out to the point guard (PG), who continues the ball around the horn to the shooting guard (SG). The center (C) fakes across the lane, then cuts hard directly toward SG. After inbounding, SF moves in to set a screen for PF. PF cuts behind the pick and moves into the lane near the baseline. Both big players are then in the lane, and SG chooses where to go with the ball (Diagram B).

Coaching Point:

- This play is designed to move very quickly. The ball movement around the horn should be as rapid as possible.

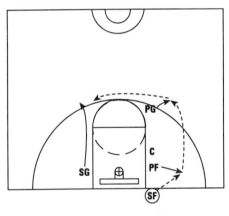

Diagram A

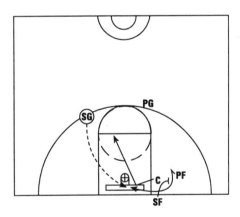

Diagram B

Drill #70: The Backwards "L" Set

Objective: To safely inbound the ball using a random set.

Description: This drill begins with the small forward (SF) inbounding the ball and the rest of the offensive players positioned as shown in Diagram A. The center (C) remains in the low post position, and the power forward (PF) breaks to the sideline to take the inbound pass. The shooting guard (SG) moves over to screen for the point guard (PG) at the same time. PG breaks to the high wing for the pass from PF, and SF clears out to the offside. After screening, SG moves to the top of the key opposite PG, and takes the pass from PG (Diagram B). PG teams up with C to set a double screen for PF. PF loops around the screen into the lane for a pass from SG. Diagram C illustrates a different version of this play. Instead of completing the reversal to SG, PG dribbles toward the top of the key to give SF time to loop around a double screen from C and PF. SF loops around the screen into the lane to receive the pass from PG.

Coaching Point:

- Rapid ball movement around the horn is the key to this play.

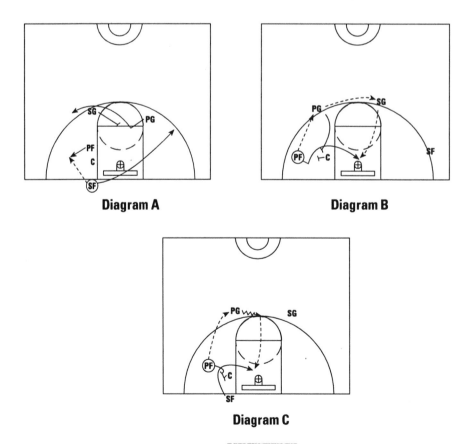

Diagram A   Diagram B

Diagram C

Drill #71: Post Up the SG

Objective: To safely inbound the ball using a random set.

Description: This play begins with the players positioned as illustrated in Diagram A. The shooting guard (SG) establishes a good post-up position at the offside lane line. The center (C) and power forward (PF) remain to the outside to leave the middle open for SG to maneuver if he gets the ball in the post. The small forward (SF) inbounds the ball to C, who passes out to the point guard (PG) at the ballside top of the key. PG dribbles toward the far side of the court looking for a chance to feed SG on the post. If the pass is not open, PF leaves the wing vacant and breaks under the basket (Diagram B). SG abandons the post position and moves under the basket to set a screen for PF, who moves back to the ballside low post looking for the feed from PG. C moves into the lane to give PF a second option. If C does not get the pass immediately, he breaks down the lane and sets a pick for SG. SG cuts off the screen and breaks up the lane for the pass and the jump-shot.

Coaching Point:

- This play is especially effective if SG is a good post-up player or enjoys a size advantage on his defender.

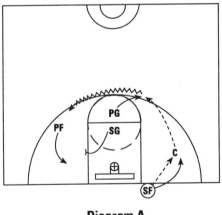

Diagram A

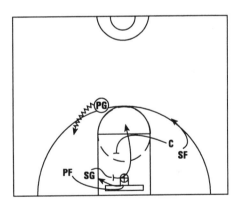

Diagram B

Drill #72: Beat the Help

Objective: To safely inbound the ball using a random set.

Description: This drill begins with the small forward (SF) inbounding the ball and the rest of the offense positioned as shown in Diagram A. The center (C) breaks up and sets a screen for the power forward (PF). PF breaks to the outside of the pick and cuts down the lane line for the inbound pass. C continues on to set a pick for the shooting guard (SG). SG follows PF off the pick by C, but breaks out to the wing instead of moving down the lane. After screening, C rolls toward the ball, giving SF a target around the foul line. The point guard (PG) has been watching the action from the ballside corner. If PG's defender sags in to help on PF's drive down the lane line, SF hits PG for the open shot. Occasionally, defenders will be instructed not to follow their opponents outside. If PF's defender sags into the middle instead of staying with PF, Diagram B illustrates an alternative play. C screens PF's defender, then rolls to the ball deep in the lane for the inbound pass. PF moves up to screen for SG, and SG cuts to the wing offering SF a second option.

Coaching Point:

- If PF's defender is cheating to the outside of C's pick, PF should break inside directly to the basket.

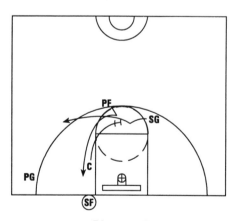

Diagram A

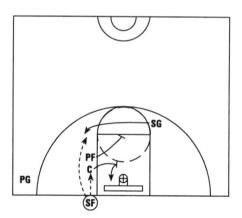

Diagram B

Drill #73: Between the Screens

Objective: To safely inbound the ball using a random set.

Description: This drill begins with the players positioned as illustrated in Diagram A. The center (C) and power forward (PF) set a double screen near the lane line. Each player attempts to set the pick in a manner that forces his defender away from the middle of the screen. The shooting guard (SG) breaks through the middle of the double screen. The small forward (SF) finds SG for what should be an open shot. If the shot is not open, SG passes outside to the point guard (PG) (Diagram B). PF screens for SF, who breaks up to the foul line after inbounding the ball. After screening, PF rolls back to the other edge of the foul line. C sets a backscreen for SF, and rolls into the lane in the position vacated by PF. This maneuver gives PG three places to go with the ball.

Coaching Point:

- C and PF must force their defenders away from the middle of the screen so SG does not get caught in traffic when he's coming through.

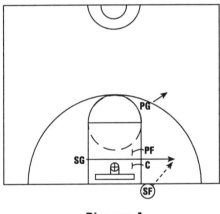

Diagram A

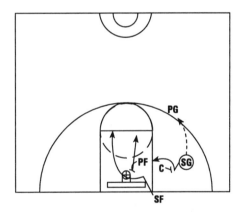

Diagram B

Drill #74: Double Screen, Double Roll

Objective: To safely inbound the ball using a random set.

Description: This drill begins with the small forward (SF) inbounding the ball and the rest of the offense positioned as illustrated in Diagram A. The post players move up the key and set screens for the shooting guard (SG) and point guard (PG). SG and PG both cut to the wings, and the center (C) and power forward (PF) roll off their picks toward the basket. If C or PF is open off the roll, SF delivers the ball. If not, the inbound pass is made to PG on the wing. When PG has the ball, both C and PF move down to screen for SF. SF reads the defense and cuts either way off the screen. PG should find SF open on the baseline or cutting up the lane. If not, C and PF post up and look for the feed from PG.

Coaching Point:

- The inbounder should be both smart and quick underneath. The coach should adjust his personnel accordingly.

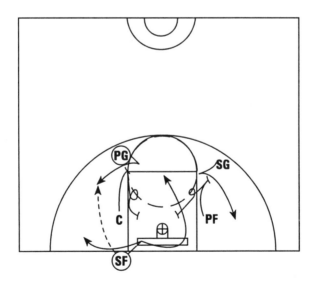

Drill #75: Time the Traffic

Objective: To safely inbound the ball using a random set.

Description: This drill begins with the ball in the small forward's (SF) hands and the other offensive players positioned as illustrated in Diagram A. The center (C) and power forward (PF) set a double screen for the shooting guard (SG) just inside the lane line. SG breaks across the lane and cuts to the wing around the outside of the screen. The point guard (PG) breaks directly down the lane toward the basket, cutting off of SG's heels. If PG is open, it should be for a lay-up. If not, PG clears out to the offside wing, and SF inbounds to SG on the wing for the outside shot. If the shot is not open, SF loops around a double screen set by C and PF to the foul line for the pass from SG and takes the jump-shot (Diagram B).

Coaching Point:

* The key to getting PG the ball for an easy lay-up is the timing of his cut off SG's break across the lane. If it is timed perfectly, PG should be able to shake his defender in the traffic.

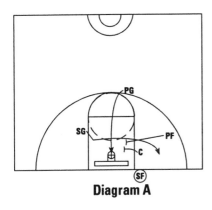
Diagram A

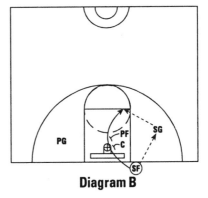
Diagram B

Drill #76: SF Learns to Read

Objective: To safely inbound the ball using a random set.

Description: This drill begins with the small forward (SF) inbounding the ball and the other offensive players positioned as shown in Diagram A. The point guard (PG) moves diagonally up through the lane and sets a screen for the shooting guard (SG). SG tries to drive his defender to the outside of the screen then cuts off the screen directly down the lane toward the basket. The power forward (PF) then moves across to set a pick for PG, who rolls off the pick out to the high wing. After screening, PF breaks diagonally down the lane to the offside low post. This maneuver gives SF two places to go with the ball. If neither is open, SF inbounds to the center (C), who has moved out to the corner (Diagram B). C passes outside to PG, then moves down to set a screen for SF. SG also sets a screen for SF. SF must read the defense and break off either screen. PG should find SF open on the baseline if he cuts off C's pick, or open coming up the lane off SG's screen.

Coaching Point:

- The double screen from SG and C should break SF free if he makes the right read.

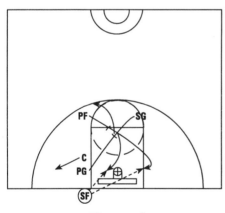

Diagram A

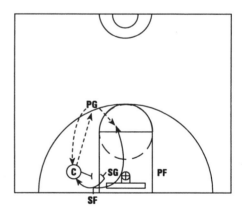

Diagram B

CHAPTER 6

SIDE-OUTS

Drill #77: Pick the Picker for SG

Objective: To safely inbound the ball in a side-out situation.

Description: This drill begins with the ball in the small forward's (SF) hands and the other offensive players positioned as shown in Diagram 77. The power forward (PF) fakes toward the baseline and breaks out to the sideline to post up. SF inbounds the ball to PF, and PF returns the pass immediately. SF begins dribbling the ball toward the opposite side of the court, and the point guard (PG) moves up to set a screen for PF. PF breaks around the screen and clears out to the offside low post, receiving a pick in the lane from the shooting guard (SG) along the way. The center (C) moves to the top of the key and screens for SF as he is dribbling cross court, then rolls down the lane and sets a pick for SG. SG breaks off C's pick toward the foul line. SF can either get the ball down low to PF, or find SG coming up the lane for the jumper.

Coaching Point:

- The series of screens in this play can easily lead to defensive miscommunication and a switch. If a switch is forced, there will almost always be a smaller defender on a bigger offensive player.

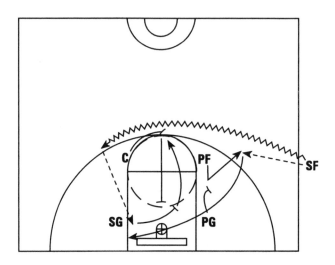

Drill #78: Take Your Pick, SF or SG

Objective: To safely inbound the ball in a side-out situation.

Description: This drill begins with the players positioned as illustrated in the diagram below. The center (C) and power forward (PF) move down to set screens for the point guard (PG). PG cuts up the lane off the screens and receives the inbound pass from the small forward (SF) on the high wing. After inbounding, SF breaks around the baseline to the opposite side with help from a screen from the shooting guard (SG). PG begins dribbling to the other side of the court. C and PF now set a double screen for SG, and SG breaks around the barricade up toward the top of the key. PG can choose between SG and SF who is breaking free from the baseline.

Coaching Point:

* The screens from the big post players are what break this play open.

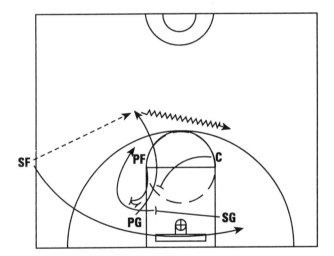

Drill #79: Side-Out to Lob

Objective: To safely inbound the ball in a side-out situation.

Description: This drill begins with the small forward (SF) inbounding the ball near half-court and the rest of the offensive players positioned as shown in the diagram below. The center (C) crosses the lane to set a pick for the point guard (PG). PG drives his defender toward the lane and then cuts outside to take the inbound pass from SF. Meanwhile, the power forward (PF) has moved across the lane to set a screen for the shooting guard (SG). SG breaks baseline off the pick to the wing, and PF rolls off the screen to the opposite wing. SF finds SG in the corner for the jumper, or passes in to PG if SG is not open. Diagram B shows the next phase of the play. PG begins dribbling the ball cross court, and C rolls off the screen he had set for PG to give a pick to SF. SF cuts off the screen and breaks to the low post to look for the ball. Meanwhile, PG has passed to PF in the corner. If C's defender is playing between C and the ball, C rolls to the hoop and pins his opponent to the outside. PF either feeds SF in the low post or, preferably, goes to C with a lob pass.

Coaching Point:

- PF must read C's defender. If the defender is playing behind C, it will be difficult for C to seal. In that case, PF should feed SF on the low post.

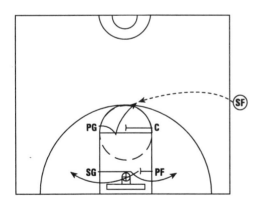

Diagram A

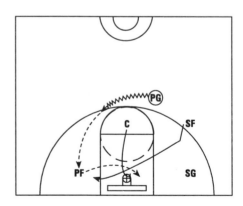

Diagram B

Drill #80: "Short Stack"

Objective: To safely inbound the ball in a side-out situation.

Description: The drill begins with the small forward (SF) inbounding the ball near half-court and the other offensive players positioned as shown in Diagram A. The shooting guard (SG) moves across the top of the key to set a pick for the point guard (PG). PG cuts off his defender and breaks to the ball to receive the inbound pass. SG cuts to the offside top of the key and takes the pass from PG. From this point on, PG functions as a safety. The center (C) and power forward (PF) are down low in a short stack, maneuvering with their defenders for position. After inbounding, SF breaks around the baseline side of the stack, leaving his defender caught in the stack. As soon as SF clears the stack, C breaks hard diagonally up the lane. SG hits SF coming clear for the jumper, or finds C coming up the lane (Diagram B).

Coaching Point:

- PF and C must keep the short stack far enough from the baseline to allow SF to pass, but close enough to pick off SF's defender.

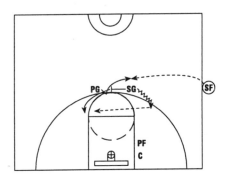

Diagram A

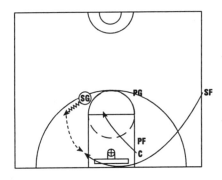

Diagram B

Drill #81: Safety First, Jump-Shot Second

Objective: To safely inbound the ball in a side-out situation.

Description: This drill begins with the players positioned as illustrated in Diagram A. The ball is inbounded quickly as the power forward (PF) sets a screen for the point guard (PG). PG breaks around the screen to receive the pass. PG then begins to dribble to the middle of the court as illustrated in Diagram B. The entire weakside of the court is cleared except for the center (C), who has moved across to the center of the lane down low. PG attempts to beat his defender one-on-one in an effort to drive down the lane to set up a two-on-two situation with C. If that doesn't work, PG passes back to the shooting guard (SG) near the top of the key. SG has broken free off a screen from the small forward (SF) and PF, and should be open for the jumper.

Coaching Point:

- This alignment spreads out the defense, making the inbound pass much safer.

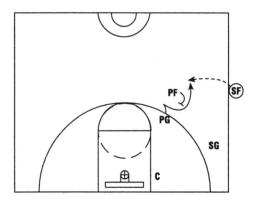

Diagram A

Diagram B

Drill #82: Five In a Line

Objective: To safely inbound the ball in a side-out situation; to practice a play designed to produce a three-point shot.

Description: The drill begins with the shooting guard (SG) inbounding the ball and the rest of the offense positioned in a straight line near half-court as illustrated in Diagram A. The point guard (PG) breaks from the end of the line and cuts around the stack toward the baseline. He should be ahead of his defender. If PG is open, SG gives up the ball immediately, and PG moves down for the quick three-point attempt. If PG does not get the ball, the small forward (SF) breaks out of the line and takes the inbound pass. The next attempt to get a three-point shot is shown in Diagram B. The power forward (PF) and center (C) step down and set a double screen. After inbounding, SG drives toward the lane to set up his defender. He then reverse cuts around the barricade to receive a pass from SF, and attempts a three-point shot if he is open. If SG cannot get the pass, C and PF move down to set a screen for PG. PG cuts off the screen back to the top of the key looking for a pass from SF to take the three-pointer.

Coaching Point:

- The best chance for an open shot is the first option. The coach should adjust his personnel so your best three-point shooter is coming off the back of the stack.

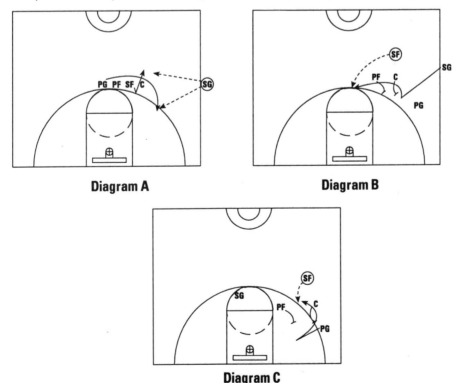

Diagram A

Diagram B

Diagram C

Drill #83: Beat the Overplay

Objective: To safely inbound the ball in a side-out situation; to provide a way to beat a defensive team that is overplaying to deny the inbound pass.

Description: The drill begins with the small forward (SF) inbounding the ball near half-court and the other offensive players positioned as shown in the diagram below. The shooting guard (SG) fakes out, attempting to get his man to overplay. SG then breaks deep down the offside of the court and may be open for a long pass. The power forward (PF) screens for the point guard (PG), who breaks around the pick toward the ball. The preferred option is for the center (C) to break quickly toward the inbounder and receive the pass with his arms fully extended. C passes quickly back to SF, who has moved toward the baseline. SF should be open to drive to the basket for a lay-up.

Coaching Point:

- This play is most effective when the ball is inbounded close to half-court, because it spreads the defense and gives SF more room to maneuver.

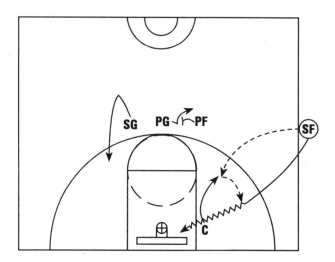

Drill #84: PF Plays PG

Objective: To safely inbound the ball in a side-out situation.

Description: The play begins with the point guard (PG) inbounding the ball near half-court and the players positioned as shown in Diagram A. The power forward (PF) fakes low, then pops out high to take the inbound pass. The center (C) moves down and sets a pick for the small forward (SF). SF cuts up to the offside wing. After inbounding, PG clears to the offside, going baseline around a screen from the shooting guard (SG) and C. If SF gets open, PF can pass quickly for the shot. PF can also choose to distribute the ball to C in the lane to create a one-on-one inside situation. After passing, PF screens down for SG, who pops off the pick for a possible pass and jump shot (Diagram B).

Coaching Point:

- PG should stay wide on the offside to open up the lane for C.

- The screen PF sets for SG is designed to keep the offside defenders from helping inside, as well as to get a shot for SG.

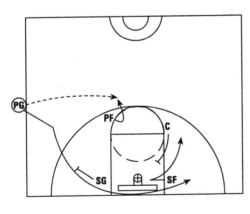

Diagram A

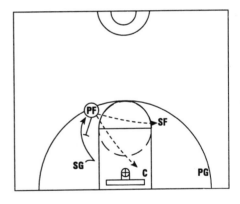

Diagram B

Drill #85: Surprise! It's a Lob

Objective: To safely inbound the ball in a side-out situation; to create a chance to score quickly using the element of surprise.

Description: This drill begins with the players positioned as illustrated in the diagram below. The shooting guard (SG) moves over and sets a pick for the point guard (PG). PG breaks off the pick toward the ball as if he were the intended target. The power forward (PF) breaks toward the ball, helping to clear out the lane. PG and PF are inbound options for the small forward (SF) if the lob isn't available. The center (C) moves up past the foul line to set a screen for SG. This maneuver also clears out the lane. SG cuts off C's screen and breaks down the lane looking for the inbound lob.

Coaching Point:

- This play must be run quickly to be effective. Everyone breaks on a signal from SF.

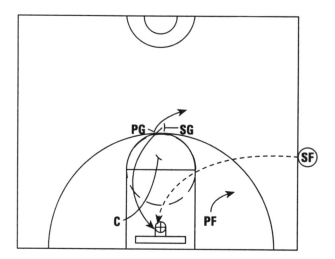

Drill #86: Isolate C

Objective: To safely inbound the ball in a side-out situation; to isolate the center in the post.

Description: This drill begins with the small forward (SF) inbounding the ball near half-court and the other players positioned as illustrated in the diagram below. The center (C) moves into the center of the lane to set a pick for the point guard (PG). PG starts toward the screen as if he is going to use it, then breaks sharply up the free throw lane line instead. The power forward (PF) moves across the lane to the elbow to set a pick for the shooting guard (SG). SG cuts off the pick toward the inbounder to take the pass from SF. PF remains in position and sets a second pick for PG as he comes up the lane to take position at the offside top of the key. After inbounding, SF stays high to act as a safety with PG. SG dribbles toward the ballside wing and passes into C, who is alone in the lane. The one-on-one post game commences.

Coaching Point:

- If C's defender overplays between the ball and C, C seals the defender, creating the opportunity for a lob pass.

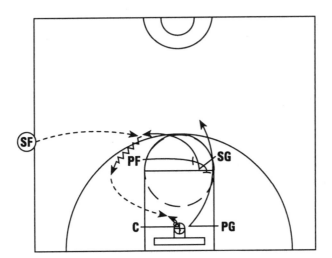

Drill #87: Lob to the Little Guy

Objective: To safely inbound the ball in a side-out situation.

Description: The drill begins with the small forward (SF) inbounding the ball near half-court and the rest of the offense positioned as shown in Diagram A. The center (C) sets a screen for the shooting guard (SG), who goes by on the baseline side to get free in the corner. The power forward (PF) moves toward the baseline and cuts diagonally through the lane toward the inbounder. The point guard (PG) fakes toward the ball and breaks down the lane after PF has cleared. All the action is now on the ballside of the court. There is no one to stop a lob pass to PG moving down the lane. PF and SG are the first options only if they break clear of their defenders. If SG gets the inbound pass and cannot shoot, he reads C's defender. If the defender was cheating on the high side to be between C and the inbounder, C seals the defender outside, and the pass comes in on the baseline.

Coaching Point:

- C should set the screen for SG far enough from the baseline to let SG through, but close enough to catch the defender in traffic.

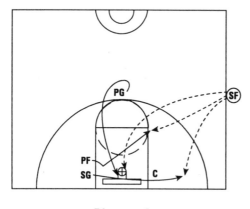

Diagram A

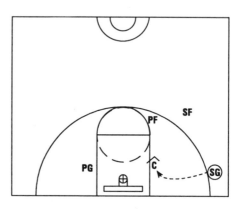

Diagram B

Drill #88: Sideline Box to the Jumper

Objective: To safely inbound the ball in a side-out situation.

Description: This drill begins with the players positioned as shown in Diagram A. The point guard (PG) breaks across the lane and sets a pick for the small forward (SF). After screening, PG continues to the offside low post. SF breaks baseline around the screen and moves to the ballside wing. The power forward (PF) steps up to receive the inbound pass and immediately passes cross court to the center (C). SF moves up from the wing to set a double screen with PF for the inbounder. The shooting guard (SG) fakes as if to break off the screen on the baseline and v-cuts around the top of the screen. C passes to SG, who takes the jumper if it is open. If it is not open, PG breaks up and sets a backscreen for C, who cuts to the basket for a pass from SG (Diagram B). In Diagram C, the ball is inbounded to PF, who passes cross court to C. Instead of screening for SF, PG breaks up and sets a backscreen for PF. SF breaks to the wing to clear the lane and take a pass from C. PF cuts off the pick through the lane for a pass from SF for an easy bucket.

Coaching Point:

- Both SG and C must sell their fakes in order to break cleanly off their screens.

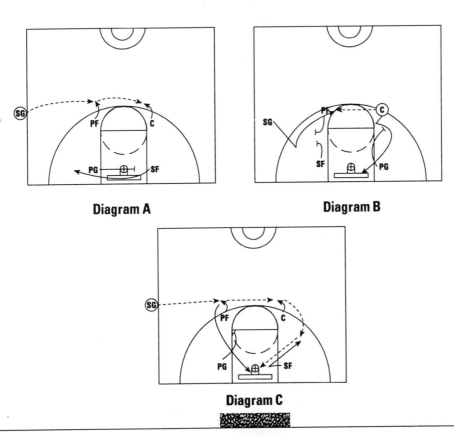

Diagram A

Diagram B

Diagram C

Drill #89: Power to Finesse

Objective: To safely inbound the ball in a side-out situation.

Description: This drill begin with the power forward (PF) inbounding the ball near half-court and the rest of the offense positioned as illustrated in Diagram A, leaving the lane and baseline open. This play is a two-phase maneuver designed to get a power drive to the basket or a clear jump-shot for a good shooter. The point guard (PG) takes a quick inbound pass from PF and immediately passes to the small forward (SF) on the offside wing. The shooting guard (SG) moves out and sets a pick on PF's defender. PF sets up his defender and cuts hard down the lane for a pass from SF. If PF is not open, the center (C) and PG move over and set a double screen for SG. SG fakes baseline and curls around the top of the screen for a pass from SF and the jump shot.

Coaching Points:

- C should act as if he is attempting to receive the inbound pass to keep his defender from sagging to the middle.

- If the screen from SF on PF's defender is a good one, PF should be free for a lay-up.

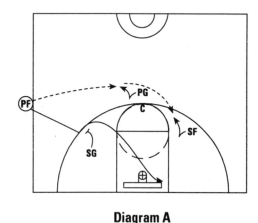

Diagram A

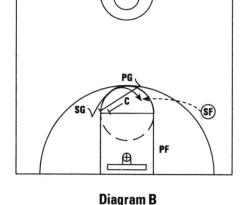

Diagram B

Drill #90: Choose the Wing

Objective: To safely inbound the ball using a box set in a side-out situation.

Description: This drill begins with the small forward (SF) inbounding the ball and the other offensive players positioned as shown in Diagram A. The power forward (PF) moves down and sets a pick for the point guard (PG). PG cuts off the screen up the lane to receive the inbound pass. As PG begins to dribble cross court, the center (C) moves down to set a screen for the shooting guard (SG). PF and SF move into position to set a series of screens for SG. SG must read the defense and choose which screen to use. SG then breaks off the pick and goes to either wing for a jump-shot.

Coaching Point:

- This play is designed to set up a team's best outside jump-shooter. A coach should adjust his personnel accordingly.

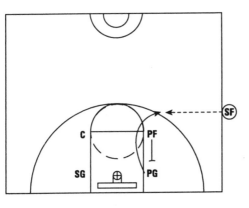

Diagram A

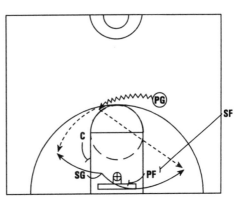

Diagram B

Drill #91: Lob to Post-Up to Jumper

Objective: To safely inbound the ball in a side-out situation.

Description: This drill begins with the players positioned as illustrated in Diagram A. The point guard (PG) breaks outside to function as the third option for the inbounder. The shooting guard (SG) breaks to the corner looking for a pass, and clears out the lane in the process. The power forward (PF) moves diagonally up across the lane and sets a screen for the center (C). C breaks around the pick and down the lane for the quick lob pass. The second option is illustrated in Diagram B. If C does not get the lob, he moves to the offside low post and establishes good post-up position. SF inbounds to PF, who looks to feed C in the low post. If PF cannot get the ball into C, he passes to PG. PG dribbles toward the wing as SG comes across the court on the baseline to the opposite corner. PG finds either C posting up or SG in the corner for the jump shot.

Coaching Point:

- If the screen by PF for C is solid, C should be open for the quick lob.

Diagram A

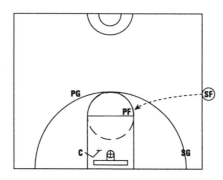

Diagram B

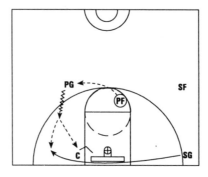

Diagram C

Drill #92: Work Low

Objective: To safely inbound the ball in a side-out situation.

Description: This drill begins with the power forward (PF) inbounding the ball and the rest of the offense positioned as shown in Diagram A. The ball is inbounded quickly to the small forward (SF), who passes to the point guard (PG). The center (C) takes three steps into the lane to allow SF time to come down and set a pick. C breaks off the pick to corner, clearing the lane. The shooting guard (SG) moves up through the lane and sets a pick for the inbounder. After screening for C, SF also gets in position to screen for PF. PF works around both screens through the lane and replaces C on the low post. PG dribbles toward the wing and passes to C in the corner. SF acts as if he is trying to post up for the pass from C, prompting SF's defender to play between SF and the ball. SF then gets position to keep the defender away from the center of the lane and looks for the lob from C.

Coaching Point:

* the timing of the maneuvers used in this play should be practiced. SF needs to come open for the lob only when the pass can be delivered, not before.

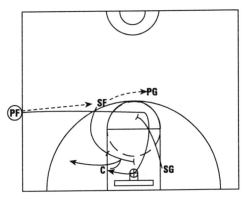

Diagram A

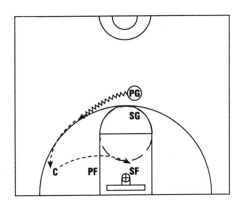

Diagram B

Drill #93: Work SF Down Low

Objective: To safely inbound the ball in a side-out situation.

Description: This drill begins with the players positioned as illustrated in Diagram A. The small forward (SF) breaks off a screen by the point guard (PG) to take the quick inbound pass. The shooting guard (SG) goes between SF and the half-court line to take the ball and begins dribbling toward the far side of the court. SF remains in position at the offside top of the key. The center (C) breaks up toward SG looking for the ball (Diagram B). At the same time, the power forward (PF) breaks up and sets a screen for SF. SG feeds C, who immediately looks for SF breaking around the screen to the basket. If the pass can be completed, a lay-up should result. If C cannot get the ball to SF, Diagram C illustrates the next option. C passes over to PF. PF feeds SF, who has battled to establish good low-post position.

Coaching Points:

- The attempt at the lay-up is a quick play that needs perfect timing.

- This play is designed to take advantage of a situation where SF enjoys a height advantage over his opponent, or where SF is an exceptionally good post player.

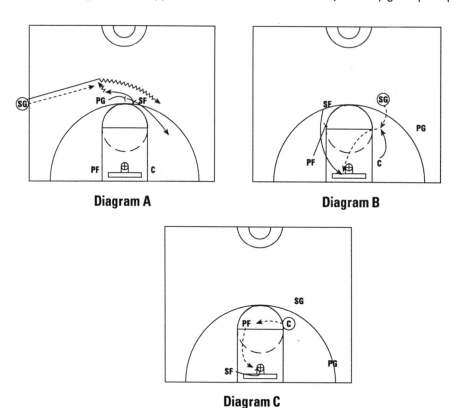

Diagram A   **Diagram B**

Diagram C

Drill #94: One Pass, One Bucket

Objective: To safely inbound the ball in a side-out situation; to work on a play that can result in a quick score.

Description: This drill begins with the small forward (SF) inbounding the ball near half-court and the other offensive players positioned as illustrated in the diagram below. The power forward (PF) breaks up toward the ball and establishes a good post-up position to receive the inbound pass. PF's objective is to clear the lane and act as a secondary inbound option for SF. The shooting guard (SG) moves across to screen for the point guard (PG), who cuts outside to serve as another secondary target for the inbounder. The center (C) breaks up the lane and sets a pick-for-the-picker near the foul line. SG rolls off his screen for PG and uses C's pick to break free down the lane for the inbound pass and lay-up.

Coaching Point:

- This play is a quick maneuver that needs work to perfect the timing.

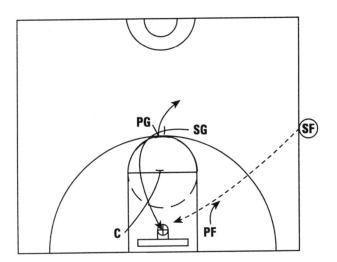

Drill #95: If At First You Don't Succeed...

Objective: To safely inbound the ball in a side-out situation; to practice a play designed to produce a lob pass leading to a score underneath.

Description: The drill begins with the players positioned as illustrated in Diagram A. The shooting guard (SG) breaks outside around the power forward (PF) and continues down, curling around the center (C). SG comes up through the lane to the offside of the foul line. PF screens for the point guard (PG), who cuts off the screen for the inbound pass. The inbounder breaks for the corner, and PG dribbles toward the wing, allowing the play to develop. C moves up the lane line toward PG as if posting up to clear his defender out of the lane. PF arcs toward the foul line, and breaks off SG's screen down the lane looking for the lob from PG (Diagram B). If that lob is not available, PG dribbles toward the top of the key, allowing time for PF to move up the lane and set a backscreen for C. C breaks to the baseline off the pick and PG looks to try a second lob pass on the play (Diagram C).

Coaching Point:

- The screens from SG and PF to spring the receivers free are the keys to success in this play.

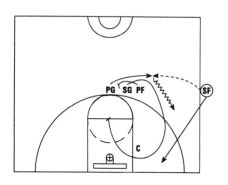

Diagram A

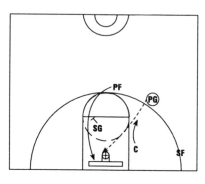

Diagram B

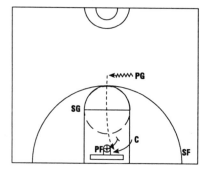

Diagram C

Drill #96: Side-Out Foul Line Stack

Objective: To safely inbound the ball in a side-out situation.

Description: This drill begins with the power forward (PF) inbounding the ball near half-court and the rest of the offensive players positioned as illustrated in Diagram A. The point guard (PG) drives his defender toward the foul line stack, then reverse cuts sharply around the barricade to the basket, looking for a pass over the top. As PG passes the stack, the center (C) and small forward (SF) set a double screen for the shooting guard (SG). SG fakes baseline and reverse-cuts around the pick to pop out for the inbound pass and the short jumper. PF looks first to PG, but shifts his attention to SG if PG is not open. If neither of the first two options is open, SG clears out down to the wing, and C sets a pick for SF. SF cuts off the screen to the top of the key, and C rolls to the ballside lane line. PF now has two more places to go with the ball (Diagram B).

Coaching Point:

- The need to do a good job setting up their defenders before cutting off the screens should be emphasized to PG and SG.

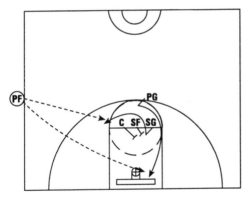

Diagram A

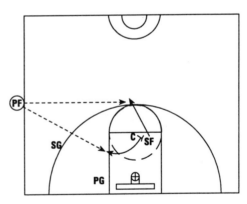

Diagram B

Drill #97: Double Screen For SG

Objective: To safely inbound the ball in a side-out situation.

Description: This drill begins with the small forward (SF) inbounding the ball near half-court and the rest of the offense positioned as shown in Diagram A. The center (C) steps into the lane to set a pick for the shooting guard (SG), who breaks across the lane and around the baseline side of the screen to the corner. C then rolls hard to the ballside elbow. The power forward (PF) breaks across and sets a screen for the point guard (PG). PG scrapes his defender off the pick and breaks out looking for the inbound pass. SF can go to any of his three teammates, but the first option is PG. C then moves up to set a screen for the inbounder as PG passes cross court to PF. SF breaks off C's pick and cuts diagonally down through the lane. If SF is free, PF delivers the ball. After passing to PF (Diagram B). PG moves down and, along with C, sets a double screen for SG, who should be open off the pick for the pass and jump shot.

Coaching Point:

- C and PG must wait until SF has cut down the lane with his defender before moving down to set the double screen.

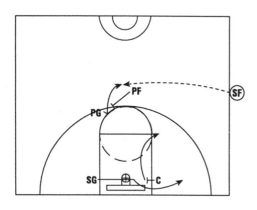

Diagram A

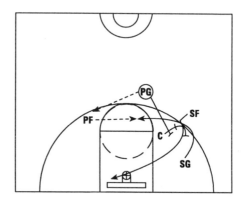

Diagram B

Drill #98: Clear the Offside

Objective: To safely inbound the ball in a side-out situation.

Description: This drill begins with the shooting guard (SG) inbounding the ball near half-court and the rest of the offensive players positioned as shown in Diagram A. The small forward (SF) sets a pick for the point guard (PG), who cuts off the screen to the ballside top of the key. After screening, SF moves to the offside top of the key. SG inbounds to PG, and the power forward (PF) clears out the offside by breaking hard to the ballside elbow. PG then passes to SF, and the inbounder breaks down to the baseline and cuts across the lane, using a screen from the center (C) to lose his defender. As SG cuts off the screen, PF is in place to pick for the picker. C curls around PF's screen to the center of the lane. SF has two players coming free in the lane from which to choose (Diagram B).

Coaching Point:

- PF must be on the move and ready to screen for C as soon as SG cuts around C's screen.

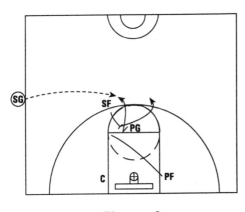

Diagram A

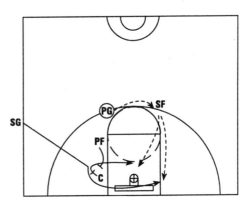

Diagram B

Drill #99: Two-Pass Lay-Up

Objective: To safely inbound the ball in a side-out situation.

Description: This drill begins with the players positioned as illustrated in Diagram A. The point guard (PG) screens away for the small forward (SF), and SF cuts off the pick to take the quick inbound pass. The shooting guard (SG) crosses to the half-court side of SF and receives the ball as he goes by. As SG dribbles cross court, the center (C) times a hard break up the lane to the foul line to arrive when SG is in the right passing position. SG feeds C the ball. Diagram B illustrates the continuing action. The power forward (PF) moves up and sets a backscreen for SF, who cuts off the pick down the lane. C gets the ball to SF in the lane for the lay-up.

Coaching Point:

- PF should arrive at the screening point as close to the time of SG's pass as possible. This play is an example of another situation where timing is critical.

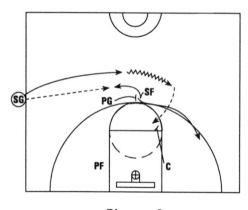

Diagram A

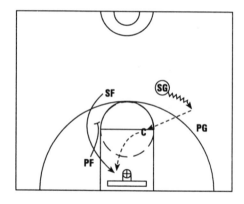

Diagram B

Drill #100: Four Choices For PG

Objective: To safely inbound the ball in a side-out situation.

Description: This drill begins with the players positioned as shown in Diagram A. The point guard (PG) breaks toward the ball and reverse cuts, clearing out to the offside wing. The center (C) and shooting guard (SG) set a double screen for the power forward (PF), who breaks around it to take the inbound pass. C stays on the perimeter and SG rolls down to the foul line. The small forward (SF) moves to the ballside wing. PF passes cross court to PG (Diagram B), then receives a pick from SG and cuts off it diagonally down the lane to the ballside low post. PG gets the ball to PF if he is open. If not, C screens for SG, who cuts off the pick to the ballside top of the key and looks for a pass from PG for the jump-shot (Diagram C). Finally, PF picks for SF, who breaks across the lane to the ballside low post. C moves to set a pick for the picker. PF breaks off the screen toward the top of the key. This gives PG two more places to pass for a scoring opportunity (Diagram D).

Coaching Points:

- Good screening technique should be emphasized.

- The drill should be run repeatedly until the players are comfortable with the flow from one option to the next.

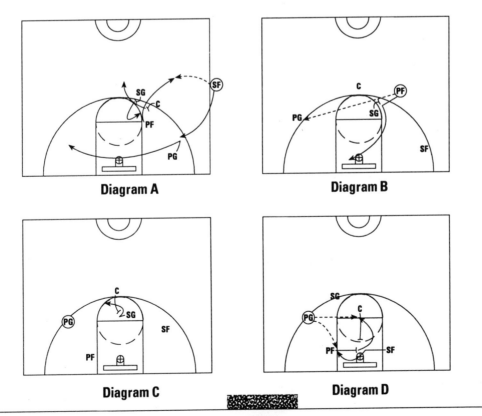

| Diagram A | Diagram B |
| Diagram C | Diagram D |

Drill #101: Side-Out One-On-One For PG

Objective: To safely inbound the ball in a side-out situation.

Description: This drill begins with the players positioned as illustrated in Diagram A. The ball is inbounded to the point guard (PG), who breaks off a pick by the power forward (PF) to get open. The PF and the shooting guard (SG) move below the foul line and set up just outside the lane in preparation for a double screen. The center (C) cuts off SG to offer a second inbound option. After inbounding, the small forward (SF) drives his defender into the double screen and cuts baseline around the pick to the offside low post. Off a screen by C, PG has been dribbling across the top of the key looking for a chance to beat his defender and drive the lane. If PG cannot shake his defender immediately, C sets another screen in an effort to shake PG loose (Diagram B).

Coaching Point:

- If PG is not successful in losing the defender, he should drive down the lane line to get the ball to SF on the low post.

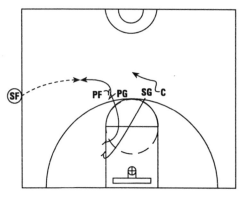

Diagram A

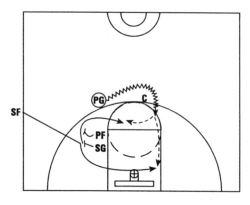

Diagram B

George Karl is the head coach of the Seattle SuperSonics. Since assuming his present position on January 23, 1992, Karl has led the Sonics to over 300 victories. A 1973 graduate of North Carolina where he played three years for Dean Smith's Tar Heels and gained All-American honors as a senior, Karl began his distinguished coaching career in 1978 as an assistant in the ABA for the San Antonio Spurs. After two seasons with the Spurs, Karl then moved to the Continental Basketball Association as the head coach of the Montana Golden Nuggets. After three years with the Golden Nuggets, he began his NBA head coaching career with the Cleveland Cavaliers in 1984. Two years later, Karl accepted the same position with the Golden State Warriors—a job he held for two seasons. Subsequently, Karl spent two additional seasons each with the CBA's Albany Patroons and with Real Madrid of the Spanish League. One of the most respected and knowledgeable coaches in the game, Karl resides in the Seattle area with his wife Cathy and their two children—Kelci and Coby.

Terry Stotts, George Karl, Price Johnson (L-R)

Jeff Reinking Photography

Terry Stotts is an assistant coach with the Seattle SuperSonics. He began his career with the Sonics in 1992 as a scout, before assuming his present position prior to the start of the 1993-94 season. A 1980 graduate of the University of Oklahoma where he earned numerous honors as a basketball player for the Sooners, Stotts began his coaching career in 1990 as an assistant coach with the Albany Patroons under current Sonic head coach George Karl. He then spent one season as an assistant with the CBA's Fort Wayne Fury, before joining the Sonics staff. Terry and his wife Jan reside in the Seattle area.

Price Johnson is a successful youth basketball coach and basketball camp director in the Bellevue, Washington area. For the past 15 years, he has worked both as coach and as advocate of youth basketball. Since 1992, Johnson has taken an all-star youth basketball team to the national tournament for youth basketball, placing in the top 10 teams each year. Johnson is a co-owner of Hoopaholics, a successful sportswear company. Price and his wife of 16 years, Julianne, reside in Bellevue, Washington with their two sons—James and Dane.

ADDITIONAL BASKETBALL RESOURCES FROM

■ *101 DEFENSIVE BASKETBALL DRILLS*
by George Karl, Terry Stotts and Price Johnson
1997 ▪ Paper ▪ 128 pp
ISBN 1-57167-079-3 ▪ $15.00

■ *101 OFFENSIVE BASKETBALL DRILLS*
by George Karl, Terry Stotts and Price Johnson
1997 ▪ Paper ▪ 120 pp
ISBN 1-57167-078-5 ▪ $15.00

■ *101 BASKETBALL REBOUNDING DRILLS*
by George Karl, Terry Stotts and Price Johnson
1997 ▪ Paper ▪ 128 pp
ISBN 1-57167-080-7 ▪ $15.00

■ *101 WOMEN'S BASKETBALL DRILLS*
by Theresa Grentz and Gary Miller
1997 ▪ Paper ▪ 128 pp
ISBN 1-57167-083-1 ▪ $15.00

■ *ATTACKING ZONE DEFENSES*
by John Kresse and Richard Jablonski
1997 ▪ Paper ▪ 128 pp
ISBN 1-57167-047-5 ▪ $15.00

TO PLACE YOUR ORDER:
U.S. customers call
TOLL FREE (800)327-5557,
or write
COACHES CHOICE Books, P.O. Box 647, Champaign, IL 61824-0647,
or FAX: (217) 359-5975